The Deconstructive Turn:

essays in the rhetoric of philosophy

The
Deconstructive Turn

*essays in the rhetoric of
philosophy*

Christopher Norris

METHUEN
London and New York

For Alison, Clare and Jenny

First published in 1983 by
Methuen & Co. Ltd
11 New Fetter Lane, London EC4P 4EE

First published in the USA in 1984 by
Methuen & Co.
in association with Methuen, Inc.
733 Third Avenue, New York, NY 10017

Typeset in Linotron 202 by
Graphicraft Typesetters Limited, Hong Kong
Printed in Great Britain by
J.W. Arrowsmith Ltd, Bristol

British Library Cataloguing in Publication Data

Norris, Christopher
The deconstructive turn.
1. *Philosophy*   2. *Rhetoric*
I. *Title*
808'0661   B52

ISBN 0-416-36140-4

Contents

Acknowledgements

The impetus for writing this book came largely from discussions carried on in the congenial but mind-stretching company of the Cardiff Critical Theory Seminar. I should also like to thank Roger Poole for his valuable comments on the Kierkegaard chapter; Richard Machin for any number of helpful suggestions; and Joseph Margolis for inviting me to speak about Wittgenstein and deconstruction on the occasion of a conference at Temple University, Philadelphia. David Woods (of the Department of Philosophy at Warwick University) offered me a lively forum for an early version of the Kierkegaard chapter. My ideas about Wittgenstein and Austin came in for much stimulating comment and debate at the School of Criticism and Theory, Northwestern University, summer 1983. To Geoffrey Hartman, Richard Rorty and Susan Shahzade – among others – I owe fond memories of a six-week intellectual haven. Terence Hawkes, more than anyone, has kept alive my interest in these matters and helped me to see, at an early stage, where my arguments were pointing.

My thanks are also due to the editors and publishers of the following journals for permission to use portions of material which first appeared in their pages: *Mind*, *The Southern Review* (Adelaide), *Philosophy and Literature*, *The Indian Journal of Applied linguistics*, *The Modern Language Review*.

Preface

I

What might be the consequences for philosophy if its texts were exposed to the kinds of reading made possible by recent developments in literary criticism? This is the question which these chapters confront from different angles and in various contexts of philosophic argument. It is the question posed most sharply by that particular practice of textual close-reading which goes under the name of deconstruction. A preface is clearly not the place to spell out the detailed arguments and strategies of deconstructionist criticism. Its effects will – I hope – become increasingly evident in the course of these chapters. However, it may be useful at this stage to offer the following brief observations as to why these particular topics were chosen, and how they relate to the concerns of philosophy and literary theory at large.

Deconstruction begins by questioning the deep laid assumption that 'philosophy' has to do with certain kinds of truth which are not to be found in 'literature'. At its simplest and most prejudicial, this attitude takes the form of Plato's belief that poetry was a kind of irrational seizure, exempt from all the curbs of wisdom and reason. Subsequent 'defences' of poetry have not so much challenged the basic Platonic position as tried to come to terms with it from a slightly different angle. Poetry offers an idealized counterpart (and hence a morally-improving alternative) to the drab realities of everyday practical experience. Such was Sir Philip Sidney's polite rejoinder to Plato in his

'*Defence of Poesie*' (1595). A Romantic like Shelley naturally pitched his claims much higher, arguing that poetry was the source and inspiration for every great advance in human society, since even science and politics had to partake of imaginative vision if their efforts were to benefit mankind. I. A. Richards' *Science and Poetry* (1925) sets out to reformulate the same basic view in modern psychological terms. Poetry is seen as an 'emotive' use of language, as opposed to the 'cognitive' or 'referential' uses available to science. And it is here precisely, according to Richards, that its unique and irreplaceable value lies. Poetry can 'save' us by preserving a region of subjectively authenticated truth immune to the encroachments of scientific method and the neutral, dehumanized world-view which goes along with it.[1]

Richards thus stands directly in the line of apologists for poetry descending from Sir Philip Sidney. Poetic language allows us to entertain *fictions* in the knowledge that they are just that, without enjoining us to believe (as religion once required) that faith could actually transcend and controvert the self-evidence of science. Richards creates a space for poetry, but only at the cost of consigning it to a specialized, 'emotive' register of language, cut off at source from any semblance of cognitive truth. This strategy assumed a more complex and sophisticated form among the American New Critics of the post-war years. Taking issue with the psychological aspect of Richards' argument – which they thought too subjective – the New Critics worked out a whole modern rhetoric of literary language designed to explain and validate its unique claims-to-truth. Their favoured poetic devices (of 'irony', 'paradox', 'ambiguity', etc.) represented a full-scale alternative programme to the scientistic view of language as a logical or referential medium. The literary critic could claim a special competence in recognizing structures of meaning and value invisible to the straight-man philosopher or scientist. But the case remained, in one sense, what it had been when Plato expelled the poets from his ideal republic. Literary language was still the determinate 'other' of science and philosophy. Its defences were still inextricably entwined with the notion that *some* kinds of language had access to a reality, or an ultimate referential grounding, which literature could never emulate. The New Critics' position would appear – from this point of view – as a grandiose defensive rationalization of their perceived disadvantage *vis-à-vis* the scientists and philosophers.

Deconstruction is perhaps most easily grasped as a move which overturns every one of those assumptions revealed in this (admittedly sketchy) historical survey. It denies, as against Plato, that philosophy has access to truths which literature can only obscure and pervert by its dissimulating play with language and fiction. It likewise undermines the very rationale of those 'defences' mounted by Sidney, Shelley and Richards. Philosophy – including the rational self-evidence of scientific thought – is always bound up with linguistic structures which crucially influence and complicate its logical workings. Philosophic texts may purport to reduce or even to exclude the vagrant, irrational effects of figurative language. Philosophers like Locke and his latter-day positivist descendents devote a great deal of their thought to establishing a discourse of dependably logical and referential meaning, such that philosophy can carry on its work undisturbed by the beguilements of rhetoric.[2] And yet – to adapt one of Bacon's sayings – 'drive metaphor out with a pitchfork, yet she will return'. Deconstruction in the hands of a conceptual rhetorician like Paul de Man shows just how omnipresent and potentially disruptive are the effects of this 'buried' figural dimension. Philosophy turns out – in de Man's reading of it – as 'an endless reflection on its own destruction at the hands of literature'.

These chapters explore the implications of opening up philosophy to various kinds of deconstructive reading. In a sense they represent the revenge of literary theory on that old tradition of philosophical disdain or condescension stretching back at least to Plato's *Republic*. But they are also intended as a reminder that deconstruction has its own kind of philosophic rigour. It can all too easily degenerate into a kind of self-admiring game if it fails to engage with texts at a level of extreme self-critical awareness. The chapters which follow are all concerned with philosophies or arguments which actively *resist* deconstruction, to the point where its effects are all the more striking for having taken hold of their text, so to speak, against all the odds.

Some examples may serve by way of brief introduction. Saul Kripke's book *Naming and Necessity* puts forward an account of language and meaning which, if accepted, would largely dissolve the much-debated problems of modern epistemology. It would also – for reasons I suggest – render deconstruction virtually redundant by providing a different, seemingly 'non-deconstructible' philosophy of language. My essay argues that the issues thus raised are strictly and rigorously *undecidable*. Kripkean semantics are indeed a perfectly logical and self-consistent alternative to the problems induced by sophisticated sceptical theories of meaning. On the other hand, Kripke's text lies open to deconstruction in certain crucial turns of argumentative strategy. Such a reading comes up against the limit-point of undecidability enforced by all self-critical reflection on the nature of language. This argument is pursued, from a somewhat different angle, in the essay on 'ordinary language' philosophy, where some texts of Gilbert Ryle are both deconstructed and seen to deconstruct – on their own terms of reference – the claims of deconstruction.

Kierkegaard presents a very different case. His writings were prompted by an overriding purpose of religious edification which could only be served, as Kierkegaard believed, by indirect means. Hence his recourse to the various devices (pseudonymous authorship, secular parables, fictional case-histories) which Kierkegaard intended as stages on the road to authentic 'inwardness' or truth. In one sense his writings pre-empt the very work of deconstruction, exhaustively rehearsing its tactics in advance. Yet they also lay claim to an ultimate justifying faith: that the reader can be led *through and beyond* these perplexities to a state of religious self-understanding vouched for elsewhere in Kierkegaard's 'authentic' texts. A deconstructive reading undermines such confident distinctions between truth and fiction, direct and indirect discourse, providential 'meaning' and the ruses which obliquely work to encompass it. The undecidability of Kierkegaard's text is such as to engender suspicions of fictional and figurative sense even in 'authentic' productions like *The Point of View for My Work as an Author*. Again, there occurs a breakdown of any possible categorical distinction between 'philosophy' and 'literature'.

The issue between Marxism and deconstruction has lately been pursued (by the Marxists at least) in a spirit of downright hostility. Terry Eagleton mounts the most articulate attack in a chapter from his book on Walter Benjamin. Deconstruction must be understood as 'an ideology of left reformism', reproducing (at the level of elaborate textual theory) those conditions of collusive failure and despair imposed upon the modern 'liberal' academic. Eagleton argues a forceful case:

> By pressing semiosis to its 'full' potential, by reading at once with and against the grain of a text that denegates its deep wounding with all the cheerful plausibility of a West Point war casualty, we can know a kind of liberation from the terrorism of meaning without having for a moment – how could we? – burst throught to an 'outside' world that could only be one more metaphysical delusion.[3]

This polemic occurs in the context of an argument expressly intended to 'rescue' Benjamin's writings for the purposes of a Marxist-materialist criticism. My own chapter on Benjamin contests what it sees as Eagleton's reductive view of deconstruction and its bearing on certain crucial ambiguities in Benjamin's work.

J. Livingston Lowes' *The Road to Xanadu* is a baggy monster of a book and, in many ways, a curiously hybrid production. It mixes an obsessive tenacity of scholarship with a dream of recreating the Romantic experience, most often through ficitions and exemplary parables of its own half-conscious engendering. Deeply suspicious of idealist metaphysics, and working for the most part with a crude associationist psychology, Lowes yet strives to articulate a kind of transcendent unifying vision, somehow vouchsafed to poet and critic alike. In the process his arguments self-deconstruct into all manner of interpretative pretexts and devices, 'allegories of reading' as de Man would call them. It offers a peculiarly rich example of the roundabout ploys to which thought may be reduced in its efforts to achieve a pure, self-authenticating access to meaning and truth.

Literary criticism is thus by no means exempt from the problems which beset philosophy in its attempt to ignore or repress the figural dimension of language. What *may* yet place the critic in a stronger (less deluded) position is the knowledge that texts are indeed rhetorical constructs, a knowledge traditionally more acceptable to literary theorists than philosophers. 'Literature turns out to be the main topic of philosophy and the

model for the kind of truth to which it aspires.' But de Man
follows up this assertion with a countervailing statement.
'When literature seduces us with the freedom of its figural
combinations, so much airier and lighter than the laboured
constructs of philosophy, it is not the less deceitful because it
asserts its own deceitful properties.'[4] Deconstruction explores
the transformative potential of treating texts as *undecidably*
situated between 'literature', 'criticism' and 'philosophy'. It
generates questions which cannot be resolved (much less dismissed) within the purely institutional bounds of any one
discipline. These chapters will have gone some way toward
achieving their purpose if they persuade the reader that *no*
privileged discourse can claim to speak the truth of its own – or
any other – textual production.

II

It has become almost a ritual gesture among writers on deconstruction to insist that what they are doing is in no sense a
species of conceptual exegesis or analysis. Deconstruction is first
and last a textual *activity*, a putting-into-question of the root
metaphysical prejudice which posits self-identical concepts outside and above the dissseminating play of language. To treat it
as amenable to handy definition is to foster a misleadingly
reductive account of that activity and hence to render one's text
redundant as it originates. On the other hand such purist
attitudes can all too easily become an excuse for mere conceptual
laziness and muddled thinking. Deconstruction has a rigour of
its own, no matter how resistant to any kind of summary
description. 'No exercise is more widespread today', writes
Derrida in *Of Grammatology*, 'and one should be able to formalize
its rules.'[5]

Just how such a 'formalization' might be achieved is not so
clear in the immediate context of Derrida's remark. It would
hardly work out as a set of logical precepts or protocols such as
might gain assent from philosophers of an 'analytic' mind.
Deconstructionist rigour – if we are to use that term – belongs to
a discourse which can only question all standard, regulative
notions of logical consistency. Nevertheless, it is hard to do
without such terms, as used to distinguish (say) a text like *Of*

Grammatology from other, looser applications of deconstructionist thinking. This is not to argue an absolute difference of kinds
between 'genuine' or philosophical deconstruction and its merely derivative or 'literary' offshoots.[6] Such distinctions, as I argue
in my 'Methodological postscript', are based on a certain policing of textual regimes, subordinating 'literature' to 'philosophy'
in a gesture which Derrida is quick to deconstruct. Yet there is, I
would claim, a demonstrable rigour at work within certain
exemplary texts of deconstruction, a cogency which need not be
invisible to those whose analytical presuppositions dispose
them to reject or ignore it. The scandal of deconstruction, simply
put, is its habit of uncovering a disjunct relationship between
logic and language, the order of concepts and the order of
signification. This can seem nothing short of scandalous to
philosophers whose primary business is the straightening out of
our conceptual endeavours through a close and rigorous attention to the workings of language. Yet it is here precisely – as
these chapters argue – that philosophy comes up against the
problems implicit in its own status as written or textual discourse. Such problems are not the peculiar province of deconstruction, to be shunted aside by analytic philosophers in the
name of good sense and reason. They are equally apparent
in texts – like those of Wittgenstein, Austin and Ryle –
which programmatically work to exclude or marginalize their
relevance.

I stress this point partly to forestall the objection that these
chapters treat of mainstream (analytic or linguistic) philosophy
from an angle wholly eccentric to its major concerns. In fact one
could argue that recent developments on the analytic front have
thrown up problems very similar to those essayed in the texts of
deconstruction. One example can be seen in the attempt of
philosophers like Quine to purge their discourse of all dependence on mentalist or *a priori* concepts and categories. For Quine,
this amounts to a vigorously anti-metaphysical programme, a
thoroughgoing pragmatism determined to break with traditional epistemology. Hence the attack (in his well-known essay
'Two dogmas of empiricism')[7] on the Kantian distinction between 'analytic' and 'synthetic' propositions, a doctrine which –
according to Quine – fails to take account of the constantly
changing relation between experience, knowledge and seeming

self-evidence. The totality of knowledge at any given time is pictured by Quine as a kind of man-made 'fabric', the edges having contact with experience while the centre is made up of what presently *count* as necessary *a priori* truths. His point is that changes on the periphery – major shifts of empirical knowledge – can always bring about a complex readjustment of truth-conditions at the centre. Logical interconnections demand that 're-evaluation of some statements entails re-evaluation of others', but the logical rules themselves are only statements within the total system, and subject also to constant revision as boundary conditions change. (See Chapter 7, p. 155ff. for further discussion of Quine's views and their place in current analytical philosophy.)

I would not want to press too far with the comparison between Derrida and Quine. The object of Quine's endeavours is a form of philosophical behaviourism intended to liberate thought from its reliance on outworn epistemological fictions. The behaviourist basis of Quine's empiricism comes across clearly in the following statement from his essay 'Things and their place in theories':

> Our talk of external things, our very notion of things, is just a conceptual apparatus that helps us to foresee and control the triggering of our sensory receptors in the light of previous triggering of our sensory receptors. The triggering, first and last, is all we have to go on.[8]

Quine's epistemological scepticism goes along with a sturdy pragmatist assumption that 'talk' links up, at least for practical purposes, with objects and events in the world outside. What he wants to bring out is the variety of possible links and the pointlessness of trying to confine them to *a priori* schemes of conceptual validity. Quine's empiricist programme could scarcely be more remote from Derrida's ceaseless undermining of any assured link between sign and referent. Nevertheless it is clear that Quine, like Derrida, perceives a covert metaphysics at work in traditional ways of conceiving philosophy; also that he shares the deconstructionist will to demystify language by removing the appeal to some ultimate ground of concept or meaning. Derrida's critique of logocentric assumptions is not, after all, so far removed from Quine's insistent refusal to entertain talk of 'meaning' outside the particular, context-governed instances of sense.

Others, after Quine, have pressed yet further in this principled mistrust of hypostatized semantic criteria. Israel Scheffler, in his book *Beyond the Letter*, provides what is perhaps the most extreme and revealing example.[9] Scheffler adopts a relentlessly nominalist approach which eschews all talk of 'meaning' or other such questionable concepts, and determines to treat of its topics (vagueness, ambiguity, metaphor) without recourse to abstract criteria. This amounts to a self-denying ordinance of extraordinary rigour and scope. Writing very much under Quine's influence, Scheffler invokes the type-token distinction (regarding 'types' as more or less abstract entities) and tries to break away from the question-begging notions of 'analyticity and synonymy, modal and counterfactual constructions, and purportedly essential features of objects or elements'.[10] To this end he proposes an 'inscriptionalist' account of natural language which takes for granted 'only the individual tokens and the individual things that may be denoted'.[11]

Scheffler's use of the term 'inscriptionalist' refers to his avowed nominalism, his claim that natural language may be clarified by an account 'taking only inscriptions as its linguistic elements and forswearing the Platonism of traditional semantics'[12] This attitude finds a distinct parallel in Derrida's critique of those philosophers, from Plato to Husserl, who have held to the notion of a 'transcendental signified' outside and beyond the play of textual signification. Of course it would be wrong to interpret Scheffler's inscriptionalist idiom as having to do with *writing* in the literal (graphic) sense of the term. What it designates – as in the usage of other analytic philosophers like Nelson Goodman[13] – is the case for restricting attention as far as possible to semantic 'tokens' rather than 'types', and for eliminating the appeal to abstract entities like images, meanings and concepts. Thus Scheffler construes Goodman's project as intended to admit 'only actual inscriptions or events, i.e. "tokens"'.[14] The instance of writing serves to focus attention on the signifier, or 'token' of meaning, in order to forestall any question-begging premature regress to the signified. Writing (or 'inscription') becomes, as it were, a generalized synecdoche employed to signal the priority accorded to token over type,

word-use in context over meaning in the abstract. The inscriptionalist idiom works to suggest that writing is the form in
which language most evidently asserts its material status, or
resists the conceptual drift from signifier to signified. Thus
Scheffler outlines his intention 'to consider in order the subjects
of ambiguity, vagueness and metaphor, seeking in each case
interpretations that will be materially adequate and will,
moreover, satisfy inscriptionalist constraints'.[15] This sense of
'material' adequacy has to do not only with the rigour of logical
argument but also with the requisite closeness to language in its
material signifying mode.

Scheffler's inscriptionalism represents the furthest extreme of
a nominalist outlook as applied to modern analytic philosophy
of language. It is also – I would argue – closely akin to certain
cardinal motives in the work of deconstruction. For Derrida, as
for Scheffler, *writing* takes on an extended significance beyond
its customary (graphic) sense. Derrida's 'proto-writing' (or *archi-
écriture*) is that which precedes and places in question the entire
structure of assumptions which govern traditional thought.
Thus it is that the texts of that tradition, as he puts it in *Of
Grammatology*,

> already give us the assured means of broaching the decon-
> struction of *the greatest totality* – the concept of the epistémé
> and logocentric metaphysics – within which are produced,
> without ever broaching the question of writing, all the
> western methods of analysis, explication, reading, or
> interpretation.[16]

Scheffler likewise proposes his inscriptionalist model of language as a means of escaping the traditional dependence on *a
priori* concepts and categories.

Of course his aim is very different from Derrida's. Scheffler
sets out to clarify natural-language phenomena by providing a
rigorously argued descriptive idiom where such phenomena
intrude as little as possible. The object, as he says, is 'to strive
for a clear, literal and precise account of such phenomena as
vagueness, ambiguity, and metaphor'.[17] Derrida would clearly
question this appeal to an order of 'literal' or primary language
supposedly capable of setting bounds to the play of figural

implication. Such metalinguistic claims to knowledge are among those characteristic philosophical moves which deconstruction most assiduously works to uncover. Thus it might be pointed out that Scheffler, in his chapter on metaphor, discusses the question of creativity in terms that are noticeably more metaphoric that his usual self-regulating habit. Metaphor 'serves often as a probe for connections that may improve understanding or spark theoretical advance'.[18] That his own theorizing might be dependent on precisely such 'natural' linguistic resources – rather than existing in a logical realm apart – is a possibility that Scheffler tries hard to exclude.

The same applies to his discussion of 'vagueness', treated as a phenomenon of natural language capable of clarification at a higher (logical) level. Thus Scheffler asserts at one point that even 'absolute vagueness' can be seen to 'evaporate as a special category' once it has been replaced by 'a contextual counterpart signifying ... a particular indecision theoretically soluble by further enquiry'.[19] To which the deconstructor might reply that Scheffler's own inscriptionalist idiom precludes such an appeal to 'context' – restrictively applied – as a means of closing off semantic possibilities. To rest his case on 'contextual counter-parts' is to fall back on something much akin to the concept of synonymy, a recourse which Scheffler – like Quine – wants to avoid.

On each of these counts – the ubiquity of metaphor and the problems of defining 'context' in relation to 'text' – deconstruction has much to say. Scheffler's resort to a restrictive notion of context would be seen as a last-ditch philosophic move to safeguard analytic reason against the disseminating play of language. The point might be made – as Derrida makes it in writing of Plato, Husserl and Saussure – that Scheffler's text provides the means of its own deconstruction by adopting an inscriptionalist idiom at odds with certain of its own, less radical working assumptions. In this respect a deconstructive reading would claim to follow through *more rigorously* the textual – if not the 'philosophical' – implications of Scheffler's argument. To draw this distinction is to note the extent to which philosophy, as an instituted discourse, works to preserve its conceptual dignity by ignoring certain aspects of its textual character. The particular interest of Scheffler's text is that its choice of an inscriptionlist idiom poses these issues in a peculiarly sharp and paradoxical form.

I have tried, through this example, to substantiate the claim that deconstruction has a rigour of its own, none the less cogent for putting into question some of the most basic assumptions of philosophic reason. The chapters in this book go on to explore the various ways in which philosophy reveals, negotiates or represses its own inescapable predicament as written language. That such problems should engage the interest of thinkers in the 'other', analytical tradition is a message which I hope will be borne out in the reading.

1

Deconstruction and 'ordinary language': speech versus writing in the text of philosophy

I

There might seem little chance of any fruitful exchange between Anglo-American philosophy of language and those developments in the wake of Saussure which currently go under the name of post-structuralism. Certainly the two traditions are worlds apart in terms of philosophical descent and governing conventions. Saussure's thinking about language can be seen as the upshot of a rationalist epistemology which – in a properly Cartesian spirit – suspends all the notions of empirical self-evidence and sets out to construct an alternative system possessed of its own internal logic.[1] This bracketing of common sense assumptions is taken as the minimal starting-point for any form of knowledge which hopes to advance beyond naïve certitude or unreflecting positivism. Such is Saussure's insistence that linguistic science be founded on a clean disciplinary break between *parole*, or the speech-stuff of everyday experience, and *langue* as the network of articulated contrasts and resemblances existing outside and beyond the speaker's immediate grasp. This act of divorce is further ratified by the 'arbitrary' nature of the sign, the fact – as Saussure argued – that there cannot exist any natural or proper relation between signifier and signified, the word as material token of meaning and the concept it conveys.

Intuition prompts us to believe otherwise, as does a whole tradition of philosophy going back at least to Plato's *Cratylus*. The 'naturalist' position comes of a sense that language, or more specifically *spoken* language, takes rise in some intimate region of awareness where meaning and thought are indissolubly merged. The idea of speech as self-presence goes along with a belief in the ability of thought to arrive at an authentic knowledge beyond reach of doubt because transparently open to inward self-scrutiny. Jacques Derrida has shown how this 'phonocentric' bias operates across the widest divergences of western philosophic thought.[2] To register the force of Derrida's critique would involve much more than simply confronting Anglo-American empiricism with yet another species of high-flown French dialectics. The point is that Derrida's techniques of deconstruction are exerted just as forcefully on Descartes, Saussure or Lévi-Strauss as on thinkers in the 'other' tradition, including – most recently – Austin and Searle. What Derrida calls the 'logocentric epoch' of western thought, and elsewhere its 'metaphysical closure', is a kind of aboriginal and endless swerve into forms of mystification so deeply ingrained that they cut across all the usual boundaries of discipline and culture.

In this, as in much besides, he carries on the Nietzschean project of unmasking the claims of systematic knowledge, showing them up as elaborate schemes for preserving and disguising the intellectual will-to-power. Derrida likewise takes over the emphasis which Nietzsche placed upon figurative language as both a source of delusion and a means – the only one available – of dismantling and exposing the ruses of philosophy. In a sentence much quoted by the current deconstructors, Nietzsche described truth as 'a mobile marching army of metaphors, metonymies and anthropomorphisms ... truths are illusions of which one has forgotten that they *are* illusions ...'.[3] Derrida applies this deconstructive insight with the added force and leverage provided by a post-Saussurean critique of the sign and its metaphysical lineage.

This is not the place for an adequate discussion of Derrida's textual strategies, as brought to bear on philosophers from Plato to Heidegger, as well as on those literary texts which he calls to witness for their power of rhetorically subverting the sovereign claim of philosophy. I have made that attempt elsewhere,[4] albeit in the knowledge of Derrida's repeated warning that deconstruction is a vigilant *activity* of thought, and not a system capable of summary description. My purpose here is to offer some comparisons, or suggestive points of contact, between Derrida's thinking and certain varieties of Anglo-American linguistic philosophy. It might appear that any such attempt must always come up against a barrier of mutual incomprehension. A gulf has seemed fixed between the two traditions, confirmed at every point by deep-grained differences in what was thought to constitute 'serious' philosophy. Attitudes to language are at the heart of this problem, increasingly so since structuralism asserted its hold over French critical thought, and British philosophy took the 'linguistic turn' which defined its modern character. On the face of it there is small hope of useful dialogue between exponents of ordinary-language philosophy and those, like Derrida, who set out to deconstruct the very notions of communicable meaning and answerable method.

There are several good reasons for revising this ostrich-like perspective. For one thing, as I have argued, Derrida's critique of western logocentrism cuts both ways. It takes in not only the 'empiricist' delusion (that knowledge of the world can be achieved undistorted by the figural snares of language), but also its 'rationalist' counterpart, that clear and distinct ideas can be arrived at by suspending reality and following the path of Cartesian principled doubt. In fact these two persuasions figure in Derrida's writing as virtual sides of a single coin, the currency of which is endlessly sustained by a constant exchange of metaphorical values. Thus Derrida can deconstruct the materialist themes of a philosopher like Condillac[5] as well as the idealist or metaphysical residues secreted in Platonic and Christian tradition. Their relationship is most pointedly defined in Derrida's several texts on Husserl and the 'phenomenological reduction'.[6] Such attempts to provide an indubitable grounding of knowledge and perception must always ignore what Derrida so shrewdly brings out, namely the *differential* structure – the alterity or radical displacement – which inhabits all meaning. Derrida presses this insight of structural linguistics to a point far beyond its methodological place in Saussure's original programme. He turns it against those philosophies of presence, from Plato to Husserl, which take as their basis an appeal to the pure self-evidence of reason. Husserl saw it as his task to ward off scepticism by providing the positivist sciences of his day with a critical or reflective grounding in transcendental logic.

Derrida's reading effectively dismantles both sides of this alliance, the pre-reflective grasp of empirical knowledge and the rationalist project which supposedly comes to its aid.

From a deconstructionist standpoint, therefore, the text-book account of philosophic history lies open to a wholesale revision which would constantly double across the boundaries of 'rationalist' and 'empiricist' thought. Richard Rorty is one of the few Anglo-American philosophers to have taken up this challenge and measured its implications. In his book *Philosophy and the Mirror of Nature* Rorty argues that the quest for knowledge and epistemological certitude has always been captive to its own engrossing metaphors. Chief among them is that of the mind as mirror, the 'glassy essence' of the soul, wherein are to be found all the representations of external reality. 'It is pictures rather than propositions, metaphors rather than statements, which determine most of our philosophical convictions.'[7] It thus becomes the task of philosophy to *legitimate* this picture of its work by repressing or forgetting the swerve into metaphor which first produced – and still sustains – its discourse. Rorty is saying, in short, that traditional epistemology rests on a mistake, a fruitful mistake in its peculiar way but one which can only lead to repeated blind-spots of paradox and error. He also makes it clear that this picture of philosophic reason is one held in common by rationalist and empiricist traditions alike. Descartes and Locke subscribe to the same great illusion, one consequence of which is the seeming exclusiveness of their two philosophies. 'It is as if the *tabula rasa* were perpetually under the gaze of the unblinking Eye of the Mind – nothing, as Descartes said, being nearer to the mind than itself.'[8] There exists a deep and systematically-misleading collusion between Lockean empiricism and the rational self-evidence of Cartesian method.

That Derrida figures only marginally in Rorty's book is no doubt a matter of strategic emphasis. He writes with Anglo-American philosophy in view, and with the principal object of weaning it away from some of its deep-laid preoccupations. To rest his case too heavily on so alien and threatening a presence would risk incurring the same response – the indifference or marginalization – which has mostly been Derrida's lot among the professional philosophers. Elsewhere, in a number of articles, Rorty has written most persuasively of Derrida's significance and the questions he poses to 'normative' or mainstream philosophy.[9] The central issue, Rorty argues, is that of philosophical *style*, in a sense more crucial and encompassing than most philosophers are willing to entertain. The resistance to deconstruction stems largely from this unwillingness. That the discipline of thought is always and everywhere bound up with a practice of style – that philosophy, as Rorty puts it, is 'a kind of writing' – cannot but seem a subversive idea to those engaged (as they believe) with pure conceptual analysis.

This is what Derrida perceives as the effect of 'logocentric' thinking down through the history of western philosophy. He sets his deconstructive sights against the ruling metaphysic which subjugates language to thought, rhetoric to logic and style to the notion of a plenitude of meaning, a pristine intelligibility immune from the effects of writing. Rorty likewise rejects the protocols of orthodox linguistic philosophy in favour of a conscious, even artful, play with stylistic possibilities. At the same time he implies that it is not just a matter of choosing one's tradition, siding (say) with Nietzsche and Heidegger as against the normative regime of stylistic repression. Rather it is a question of seeing that *both* these options come down to a choice of philosophic style, a commitment to certain operative metaphors and modes of representation. The difference then lies in the extent to which the thinker either elects to ignore or actively embraces and exploits this universal predicament.

Rorty's suggestions help to prepare for what may yet turn out to be a profitable exchange between deconstruction and the issues thrown up by recent linguistic philosophy. The point can be made from a slightly different angle by taking up his tentative distinction between 'normal' and 'abnormal' styles of philosophic discourse. 'Normal' philosophy proceeds on the assumption that knowledge is a business of orderly and systematic thinking, an enterprise built upon firm foundations of rational enquiry. Descartes, Kant and the logical positivists are among the chief examplars of this long tradition. 'Abnormal' philosophy, on the other hand, rejects the appeal of absolute knowledge and sets up to demonstrate – by various means – the delusions of systematic method. Kierkegaard, Nietzsche and Derrida stand as clear examples of this dissident tradition, with Hegel as a more ambiguous figure, torn between the claims of system and the drive toward deconstructing all systems other than his own. The hallmarks of 'abnormal' philosophy are a conscious virtuosity of style, a constant dealing in paradox and a will to problematize the relation between language and thought. The corresponding features of its normative counterpart are a disregard of style except as a means of efficient communication; a mistrust of paradox unless firmly held within argumentative bounds; and a belief that language can and should faithfully reflect the processes of thought.

II

It would clearly be misleading to set up 'linguistic philosophy' as if that term denoted a single or well-defined body of opinion. The debate has been mainly between those (like J. L. Austin) who repose their confidence in the wisdom and sufficiency of ordinary language, and those who look beyond it for some logic or conceptual grammar redeemed from its natural imprecision. Wittgenstein of course faced about in mid-career from a logical-analytic standpoint to one which acknowledged the sanctions of ordinary usage and the various ways in which language makes sense apart from the requirements of strict propositional logic. This latter persuasion was erected by Austin and his followers into a high point of principle, a belief that the perennial problems of philosophy could be conjured away by meticulous attention to the unnoticed subtleties of everyday usage.

At the same time there were those, like Gilbert Ryle, who adopted a kind of midway position, attending to the habits and conventions of 'ordinary language' but quick to point out where they generated symptoms of conceptual strain or paradox. Such are the 'category mistakes' which Ryle detects behind various cases of misleading common usage. His attempt to exorcise 'the ghost in the machine', the concept of mind as a disembodied realm of obscure private happenings, is a clear case in point.[10] It represents not only an attack on Cartesian dualism but a principled refusal to go along with normal and intuitive ways of expressing the mind-body distinction. Common usage for Ryle has nothing like the sacrosanct authority and wisdom that Austin would accord it. The bewitchment of intelligence which

Wittgenstein blamed upon the specialized jargon of philosophy can equally result from ordinary language with its unexamined bases in metaphor and myth. His distinctive style, with its fondness for paradox and homely but unsettling examples, is typical of Ryle's ambivalent attitiude toward commonsense or everyday usage.

There is, I would suggest, a very real affinity between Ryle's philosophy and Derrida's practice of textual deconstruction. They both start out from the assumption that language often runs into blind-spots of paradox – *aporia* in Derrida's Aristotelian terminology – which prevent it from effectually meaning what it says, or saying what it means. Logic, grammar and rhetoric are not simply different aspects of language but disjunct dimensions which can enter into conflict and radically undermine each other's authority. Paul de Man puts the case most succinctly in his book *Allegories of Reading*:

> The grammatical model . . . becomes rhetorical not when we have, on the one hand, a literal meaning and on the other hand a figural meaning, but when it is impossible to decide by grammatical or other linguistic devices which of the two meanings (that can be entirely incompatible) prevails. Rhetoric radically suspends logic and opens up vertiginous possibilities of referential aberration.[11]

De Man goes on to discuss the tension between 'constative' and 'performative' language in various writers from Rousseau to Nietzsche and Proust. His argument is that meaning is always undone by the radical uncertainty which leaves it suspended between statement and suasion, logical form and rhetorical force. Furthermore, this predicament can only be described in a language of analytic form which apparently *states* the deconstructionist case, and thus falls prey to its own critique, as yet another case of rhetorical doubling and delusion. The most one can achieve is to recognize – like Nietzsche, or indeed the 'early' Wittgenstein – that language cannot both *say* and *show* what it means. 'Considered as persuasion, rhetoric is performative but when considered as a system of tropes, it deconstructs its own performance.'[12]

Ryle sees philosophy in a similar light as the seeking-out of paradox, or blocks to understanding, by a process of linguistic critique. On the other hand it would clearly be unwise to press this analogy too far. Ryle is basically a commonsense philosopher, turning up problems in the conduct of language but always with a view to sorting them out and avoiding needless mystification. In Rorty's terms his discourse belongs to the 'normal' or rational-constructive tradition, making use of such 'abnormal' instances as serve to reinforce this guiding principle. De Man, like Derrida, pitches his critique at a very different level, arguing that language always and inevitably falls into traps of its own metaphysical engendering. From his Nietzschean perspective logic itself is called into doubt by the deconstructive questioning which treats all claims to knowledge as products of a rhetorical will-to-power. All the same, with these essential qualifications in mind, there is still sufficient ground for comparing the two epistemologies and pursuing what might be seen as a belated encounter.

Ryle's preoccupations are set out most clearly in his essay 'Philosophical arguments', delivered as an inaugural lecture at Oxford in 1946.[13] It is in large part a ground-clearing exercise, intended to justify philosophy as a discipline of thought with its own distinct procedures and protocols of validating argument. Ryle had already made the passage from an interest in modern continental thought (early reviews of Husserl and Heidegger) to a brief involvement with logical positivism. This background – or the effort to escape from it – is evident in the way he now tries to formulate the proper concerns of philosophy. Positivism, by its rigorous dealing with the truth-claims of science, has 'posed in a bright if painful light the corresponding question about the foundations of philosophical doctrines'.[14] Ryle had come to believe that this scientistic outlook afforded small room for real philosophical enquiry, restricting it to a mere policing of bounds laid down by the principle of positivist verification. On the other hand he had clearly absorbed its lessons to the extent of mistrusting any kind of language open to the positivist charge of empty metaphysics.

The upshot of this dual reaction is Ryle's view of philosophy as a matter of driving home the 'absurd' or unworkable conclusions resulting from mistaken linguistic implications. The object is not simply – as with Austin – to unpack the hidden assumptions of a given piece of language, but to press them to a point where they visibly buckle under the strain of their own (hitherto unnoticed) ambiguities. In this sense Ryle is a deconstructor of ordinary-language philosophy. Ideas are the product of complex propositional attitudes which exist, as it were, in compacted form and thus create confusion when their logical entailments are ignored or repressed. Commonsense linguistic knowledge has only a partial awareness of this underlying grammar. People may often be 'taken by surprise by some of the remoter logical connections of their most ordinary propositions'.[15] It is thus the philosopher's task to practise a form of *reductio ad absurdum*, drawing out the hidden contradictions of commonsense usage.

Ryle's account of this procedure could well be adapted to the defence of conceptual rhetoricians like Derrida and de Man. The most frequent charge against deconstruction is that it merely takes texts apart in a spirit of perverse and negative zeal. The analogy Ryle suggests is that of the structural engineer whose tests are likewise carried out at the physical limits of tolerance exhibited by his material:

> Certainly engineers stretch, twist, compress and batter bits of metal until they collapse, but it is just by such tests that they determine the strains which the metal will withstand. In somewhat the same way, philosophical arguments bring out the logical powers of the ideas under investigation, by fixing the precise forms of logical mishandling under which they refuse to work.[16]

Ryle's procedures are built upon this sense of language as a multiform and tensile medium, and philosophy as the deconstructive lever which raises that tension to breaking-point. It is an attitude fairly remote from the style of quizzical teasing and probing which Austin brings to bear on his items of linguistic evidence. Ryle furthermore draws a line between what he calls the 'weak' and 'strong' deployments of reductionist argument. The former require a demonstration of logical conflict within the pre-given framework and assumptions of an axiomatic system, like that of Euclidian geometry. The latter involve a more radical *aporia*, a drawing-out of corollary statements which contradict not only each other but – as Ryle would have it – the nature of reason itself.

Derrida's textual strategies are yet more extreme in the sense that they deny, or work to undermine, such appeals to a validating rational order of thought. Deconstruction sees the lure of metaphysics in all philosophies which pin their faith to an absolute Reason conceived as prior to the textual activity which articulates its working. For Derrida, the 'closure' of philosophic concepts – their absorption into structures of formalized or systematic knowledge – is always the sovereign gesture of logocentric thought. It is from this point of view that he can argue, in an essay on Husserl, that structuralism and phenomenology both partake of the same nostalgic craving for presence and certainty. It would not, he suggests, be difficult to show 'that a certain structuralism has always been philosophy's most spontaneous gesture'.[17] The Husserlian project seeks a grounding for legitimate knowledge in the notion of a self-present consciousness fully possessed of its own conceptual genesis. Structuralism supposedly rejects this approach in favour of a purely 'synchronic', objective or non-genetic method. Yet, as Derrida argues, 'it is always something like an *opening* which will frustrate the structuralist project. What I can never understand, in a structure, is that by means of which it is not closed.'[18] The two philosophies are not so much at odds as caught up in a shuttling exchange of priorities which makes it impossible to conceive of one without the other. What deconstruction must keep in view, Derrida writes, is 'the principled, essential and structural impossibility of closing a structural phenomenology'.[19]

There is a parallel here with Ryle's special view of the philosopher's predicament, caught between the transcendental claims of metaphysics and the narrowing compass of logical positivism. His early reading of Husserl and Heidegger perhaps left its mark on a style of linguistic analysis decidedly different, in idiom and conceptual reach, from the mainstream British variety. Ryle's encounter with phenomenology can be seen as a definite step toward his later rejection of Cartesian dualism and 'the ghost in the machine'. His essay on Husserl takes issue with the notion that philosophy can return to first principles by a species of 'eidetic inspection', or by turning the mind inward upon its own ideas as a test of their ultimate validity. The concepts in question, he goes on to argue, are not to be regarded as mysterious entities in some shadowy realm of private intuition. They exist only by virtue of the *uses* – intelligent or otherwise – to which they are put in philosophic discourse. Conceptual terms are 'syncategorematic', characterized by a logical grammar which governs their various entailments and their ways of meshing with a larger context of argument. Phenomenology, therefore, is on the wrong track, and headed for a form of metaphysical bewitchment, if it claims to be a privileged method of 'intuiting essences'. It can only make use of the linguistic-conceptual procedures 'by which all good philosophers have always advanced the elucidation of concepts, including consciousness-concepts'.[20] To this extent Ryle, like Derrida, rejects the idea of any privileged access to the self-present consciousness of thought.

It is therefore accurate to say that Ryle's critique of Husserl fastens upon the logocentric merging of reason and reflexive self-evidence which Derrida likewise seeks to deconstruct. Ryle detects a similar slippage into metaphor behind Heidegger's claim to have reopened for philosophy the great inaugural question of 'the Meaning of Being'. What this programme involves, in Ryle's view, is a covert smuggling of 'humanist' and 'metaphysical' motives into the first-order process of eidetic reflection. Heidegger's analyses turn out to rest on certain presuppositions about the nature of experience and the quality of that primordial Being which eludes the philosopher's conceptual grasp. It is by this means, according to Ryle, that a whole metaphysics and humanist anthropology is foisted on to the methods of Husserlian reduction. These programmatic elements 'appear to be derived from views interpolated into and not won by the Phenomenological Method'.[21]

Ryle objects to the hegemonic claim of this 'expanded' phenomenology, one which would make it 'the logical *prius*' of philosophy, science and all the branches of human knowledge. The relation between Derrida and Heidegger is of course much closer, since deconstruction takes a lead from the techniques of dismantling philosophic concepts which Heidegger saw as the only response to a bankrupt metaphysical tradition. Some of Derrida's most characteristic gestures derive from Heidegger's example. Such is the practice of employing questionable concepts but placing them 'under erasure', either typographically – by crossing them through on the page – or by devising paradoxical terms which cannot be reduced to a stable order of meaning. Derrida has coined a whole series of these deconstructive key-words, among them 'supplement', 'trace' and 'differance', the latter, by its anomalous spelling, suspended between the two French meanings 'difference' and 'deferral'. They are all designed to disrupt the conceptual economy of language by showing how meaning can fail to coincide with itself, destroying the illusion of a natural or metaphysical bond between signifier and signified.

In this respect there is a clear enough link between Derridean deconstruction and Heidegger's attempt to dismantle the history of western metaphysics. Yet Derrida typically cancels or reverses the debt by questioning Heidegger's own metaphysical motives, his quest for a grounding philosophy which would point the way back toward primordial Being. This nostalgic attachment to a lost or forgotten origin is, according to Derrida, the hallmark of all metaphysics. It operates most often in alliance with the logocentric prejudice which exalts speech as the bearer of authentic meaning, and degrades writing as a devious, parasitical or downright subversive medium. Derrida finds this conceptual formation still powerfully at work in Heidegger's texts, despite the latter's claim to have broken decisively with all such metaphysical residues. Thus when Heidegger puts forward a reading of Nietzsche as 'the last metaphysician', Derrida can shrewdly turn back his argument by pointing out that Nietzsche has anticipated any such critique through rhetorically deconstructing all claims to knowledge, his own included. It is Heidegger's quest for meaning and authenticity – his entire philosophical hermeneutic – which thus becomes the target of Derrida's Nietzschean critique.[22]

Despite his mainly sceptical response, Ryle's encounter with phenomenology seems to have exercised a complex and lasting influence, one which set his thinking firmly apart from the mainstream of ordinary-language philosophy. On the one hand it roused his suspicion of the covert metaphysics involved in any appeal to reflective self-evidence or eidetic intuition. On the other it left him dissatisfied with any logical or formalist reduction which failed to take account of the distinctive behaviour of 'consciousness-terms' in philosophic discourse. That Ryle's response is very different from Derrida's I would certainly not wish to deny. What is striking is their common perception of the problems which combine to demand this choice of alternative strategies. One further example may help to bring these problems into focus.

III

In 1960 Ryle published his essay 'Letters and syllables in Plato'. It is very much in line with his later philosophical interests, picking up several of the themes under discussion here, particularly those of 'logical grammar' and the various kinds of conceptual 'fit' between words and their contexts. Ryle pursues an analogy to be found in Plato's later dialogues, including the *Theaetetus* and *Sophist*. This is the notion that thoughts are built up in propositional form somewhat after the manner of letters combining to create a syllable, a unit of articulate sound whose properties are *not* simply the sum of its parts. In the same way, Ryle argues, concepts are always involved in a larger propositional meaning which transcends, and makes it impossible to delimit, any singular idea they might carry. The point is brought out in the following passage:

> Nouns and verbs, like consonants and vowels, can vary independently, but they cannot function by themselves. As an integral sentence is the minimum vehicle of a truth or falsehood, it is also the minimum expression of knowledge, belief and conjecture. A noun by itself or a verb by itself does not convey what I know or think, any more than a consonant-character stands for something that I can pronounce.[23]

The analogy thus lends striking support to Ryle's idea of concepts as possessing a logical power, or grammar of entailment, beyond any account that could possibly be given of their atomistic meaning.

There is another line of argument in his essay which brings it squarely into conflict with Derrida's treatment of the speech/writing opposition. For Derrida this issue is raised in exemplary form by Plato's insistence (in the *Phaedrus* and elsewhere) that speech is the only authentic medium of language, and writing merely a debased and derivative function, substituting lifeless signs for the ideal self-present unity of thought and speech.[24]

This prejudice has sometimes been explained in historical terms. It may have to do with the fact that writing was a recent acquisition in Greek culture, and one which Plato feared for its possible subversive effect in spreading novel ideas abroad. But Derrida is unconcerned with such accidents of time and place. In his view the privilege of speech over writing is the logocentric gesture *par excellence*, one which determines the course of western metaphysics and its countless subsequent attempts to close or regulate the domain of knowledge. His object, as always, is to show that writing remains a problematic and obsessive theme, even where its workings are most cunningly disguised. This 'return of the repressed' is what Derrida elicits from the figurative texture of Plato's dialogues.

Ryle argues to opposite effect that the letters and syllables of Plato's analogy must be thought of as *spoken* rather than *written* elements, 'pronounceables' and not 'inscribables'. His essay provides an almost uncanny confirmation of the link which Derrida perceives between the 'phonocentric' bias and the rationalist assumptions of philosophic thought. It is obvious enough why Ryle's line of argument demands this particular interpretation of Plato's analogy. There are, he points out, some important differences between graphic and vocal characters, such as would crucially affect the force of his argument:

> The written word 'box' contains three parts or components, namely, the 'b' and 'o' and 'x', any of which could survive when the other two were deleted.... Characters are separate inscribables; they can be separately read; and they can be combined in any order or left uncombined. But what, in the phonetic field, the three characters stand for could not be similarly separated or shuffled. We could not make a noise at all answering to the sequence of the three characters 'OXB'.[25]

A classic example, Derrida might say, of philosophy working to carve out a space for its own indispensable presuppositions. Ryle's phonocentric reading of Plato is vital to his case for pursuing the analogy between the way in which words are built up and the way in which concepts function as parts of a larger propositional context. If it could ever be shown conclusively that Plato had only written characters in mind, then the case would either collapse or require extensive reworking of the basic analogy.

It is worth noting that Ryle maintains his position against considerable odds. He needs to disregard not only the weight of scholarly opinion but also the *prima facie* argument that Plato nowhere states or suggests that he is 'talking phonetics and not graphology'. In fact what Ryle would seem to be doing is a kind of elective conceptual revision, drawing out what Plato *must be interpreted* to mean if his analogy is to hold much interest. Various details of argument and phrasing point to this revision-ist intention. The phonetic version, if true, would provide 'an almost perfect model' by which to express the context-dependent or syncategorematic nature of concept-terms. Ryle hopes that it is so, 'since the semantic view which results is both true and important'. It is hard to resist the Derridean conclusion that Ryle is here concerned with restoring a phonocentric theme to texts which not only fail to state but in some ways actively resist it. 'What I vainly wish he had said explicitly is this ...'[26]

Ryle's phonocentrism is also very much in evidence when he comes to explain how the analogy works at the level of concep-tual analysis. Derrida has pointed out the close connection between metaphors of speech-as-presence and the strategy which opposes 'live' or 'vital' language to the dead letter of script.[27] Ryle's essay makes constant use of this thematic opposition, mostly by way of underlining the difference be-tween words as isolated, empty units and the meaning they assume in the context of logical grammar. The following passage is positively laden with phonocentric metaphors and images:

> Live verbs unmistakably advertise themselves as being cores cut out of full sentences. To ask what a given live verb means is to ask what a speaker would be saying if he said something with it. Live verbs are snatches from speech, that is, from the *using* of words. Live verbs could not feature in lists. They occur only in contexts; indeed they are the lifebreath of those contexts.[28]

There could scarcely be found a more pregnant example of the figurative loading and evaluative marking of terms which de-construction sees everywhere at work. Meaning is envisaged as

the animating presence which restores mere signs to a condition
of healthy reciprocity by replacing them within the vitalizing
context of speech. It is furthermore the 'lifebreath' of linguistic
being, a metaphor which – as Derrida shows – reaches back to
the beginnings of Platonist and Christian traditions alike.
Speech is the authentic soul of language, and writing – or the
discrete characters of script – a threat to its proper mode of
being.

The opposition between 'context' and 'list' is equally crucial to
Ryle's line of argument. 'Live verbs could not feature in lists'
because any such imposed taxonomy would capture only their
lifeless written form and nothing of their vital contextualized
meaning. The discrete letters of writing may be listed in arbitrary sequence without infringing their sense, but not so the
elements of spoken language, whose meaning is invested in a
pattern of phonemic relationships within the word. Concepts
likewise are meaningless apart from the contextual ties and
entailments which determine their logical grammar. To 'list' the
extractable elements of language is to deconstruct its self-
possessed meaning into a form of resistant textual *bricolage*
which ignores all the rules of normal intelligibility. Hence the
opposite thrust of Derrida's arguments, his seemingly perverse
insistence on cleaving *to the letter* of the text, forcing it to
reveal those blind-spots of language where writing has been
repressed.

Derrida's critique of phonocentrism extends, as we have seen,
to modern structuralist theory as developed by Saussure and
his disciples. What Derrida rejects in Saussure's linguistic programme is a lingering attachment to the ethos of speech and
self-presence, with the corresponding tendency to derogate
writing as a lesser and problematic medium.[29] The exemplary
value of Saussure's texts lies in the fact that they supply all the
means and materials of their own deconstruction. Saussure
based his thinking on the principle that language was entirely
made up of signifying contrasts, or structures of difference, such
that concepts could never exist in a simple or one-to-one relation
with words. Yet, as Derrida notes, this principle is oddly
compromised when Saussure comes to reflect on the primacy of
speech and the secondary character of writing. In effect Saussure abandons – if only momentarily – his notion of the

'arbitrary' sign, and slips into a different and wholly incompatible theory of meaning. It is thus possible for Derrida to argue that Saussure's best insights are those which work to undermine his own residual attachment to the phonocentric logos. The upshot is a far more radical understanding of difference, one which can only find adequate scope in the notion of a generalized *writing* which everywhere intrudes between sound and sense, signifier and signified. The 'supplement' of writing – or difference itself – seems to haunt and frustrate every move to contain it.

Ryle's essay ventures onto the same difficult ground when it comes to explain the linguistic analogy in somewhat more concrete terms. Again, the passage needs quoting at length:

> As the atoms of writing do not stand for atoms of noise, so the atoms of speech do not stand for atoms of meaning. Conversely, as an atom of writing – a character – does stand for a respect in which one uttered monosyllable may resemble other monosyllables, while differing from them in other respects; so an atom of speech – a word – does stand for a respect in which one statable truth or falsehood may resemble others, while differing from them in other respects.[30]

It is a singularly awkward piece of text and one which, on careful reading, seems not to do quite what Ryle requires of it. His appeal to the phoneme as a minimal distinctive element of language leads on necessarily to the principle of *difference* – or the complex play of resemblance and constrast – underlying the production of meaning. But this idea carries along with it a second, covert appeal, one which in effect makes the whole passage depend on *writing* as the source of its argumentative strategy. The two main parallel constructions ('as ... so') both start out from the analogy with writing and retain from it the notion of a differential structure endemic to spoken as well as to written language. What the passage *tries* to do is progress by analogical stages from an atomistic concept of sound and meaning to a notion of them as grounded in logical grammar, itself backed up by the elaborated model of linguistic structure. What it actually *performs*, in textual terms, is a backwards unravelling of its own apparent logic, since the constant reversion to writing and difference undercuts each stage of the argument. The propositional functions of Ryle's last clause ('stable truth or falsehood') are seen to derive not from speech as the guarantee of meaning and truth, but from writing as its shunned yet ubiquitous shadow.

IV

This chapter has argued for a new way of looking at the relation between French and Anglo-American philosophy of language. It has not tried to suggest (absurdly) that they are the same activity under different names, or (perversely) that they pursue different problems to a similar conclusion. The example of Ryle is sufficient to show how wide are the divergences of method and motive which exist between the two philosophies. On the other hand there is no need to assume that this distance precludes the kind of mutual interrogative exchange which I have here sketched in outline. Deconstruction is a challenge which bears upon philosophy at points where its normative assumptions run deepest and can only be questioned – or dislodged – by a radical shift of view.

There is no real sense of intellectual engagement in the one such encounter to date, that between Derrida and John R. Searle in the pages of *Glyph*.[31] Derrida had published an essay on Austin, deconstructing the premises of speech-act philosophy and questioning the very notion of performative utterance. As might be expected Derrida seizes on the idea that speech-acts carry along with them a kind of authenticating presence, a readiness – on the speaker's part – to honour the commitments they entail. This falls plump into Derrida's sights as a case of the deluded belief that language is (properly or essentially) a medium adapted to straightforward self-expression. *Meaning what one says* is the basic condition of speech-act commitment. But what if the case were otherwise, Derrida asks, and language turned out to rest on arbitrary conventions – among them those of performative utterance – whose binding force was a mere social fiction?

Derrida concentrates his attack on the 'iterability' of speech-act forms, the fact that they must hold good for an infinite variety of possible contexts and situations. This would suggest that their force is indeed a matter of token convention and in no way tied to the sincerity or present good faith of a speaker.

Performatives therefore lose their claim to exist in some unique relation to the present activity of naming, promising, etc. Their arbitrary status, or 'iterability', places them within the public domain of language where belief in their peculiar efficacy can only be a matter of conventional assent. Derrida produces a number of supporting arguments, one of which nicely exemplifies his case. Austin is obliged to exclude from 'serious' consideration any instance of speech-act usage which manifestly fails to meet the requirement of meaning what it says. This would include such cases as promises uttered in jest, in a novel, as part of a stage dialogue or by way of second-hand quotation. Derrida characteristically fastens on these 'marginal' instances and uses them to deconstruct the claims advanced for 'normal' speech-act commitment. The same applies to Austin's exclusion of quoted speech or pieces of language deliberately lifted out of context. A 'generalized citationality' is, Derrida argues, the very condition of language, and not – as Austin would have it – a freakish departure from the norm.

Searle's response is a mixture of bafflement, exasperation and straightforward restatement of Austin's original position. He argues that the 'iterable' character of speech-acts is precisely what enables them to function properly in various contexts, since the surface regularity of form guarantees an understanding of their deeper import. He likewise protests that Derrida has wrought a mischievous perversion of commonsense reason by denying the derivative or 'parasitic' nature of quotations, fictional speech-acts and so forth. Searle's position is maintained in the perfect assurance that Derrida can only want to raise these imaginary problems through having more or less deliberately *misunderstood* the logic of Austin's intentions.

But of course this appeal to intentions and faithful understanding plays straight into Derrida's hands. His reply to Searle makes light of the notion that a text (Austin's or any other) can be grasped and comprehended to such an extent as to yield the interpreter a kind of proprietory claim. Searle attacks Derrida's 'misunderstandings', his 'falsification' of speech-act philosophy and his apparent indifference to the fact that 'Derrida's Austin ... bears almost no relation to the original'. But this is to beg the question by interpreting Austin wholly in accordance with his own professed philosophy of meaning. That is, it assumes the possibility of knowing what Austin 'originally' meant, as if somehow the author's presence lived on to validate certain readings and discountenance those that offended his sovereign will. And Searle in his turn sets up – Derrida suggests – as the sole legatee and custodian of Austin's truth, exerting the same proprietory hold and power of summary dismissal.

Derrida contests this authority by playing all manner of textual games with Searle's rejoinder. These are mostly designed to drive home the point about 'citationality' and its disturbing effects on the ethos of speech-act theory. Thus Derrida manages to quote the *entirety* of Searle's 'original' text, though always in the form of disconnected fragments which take on an alien significance at odds with their (presumed) intention. He also makes considerable play with the idea of copyright, treating it as one more proprietory ploy in the effort to safeguard texts against the violence of misinterpretation. Searle's very name is acronymically distorted and subjected to punning variations, as if to dispel the logocentric mystique which sets the author up as sovereign disposer of the text. In short, Derrida uses every possible means to break down the myth of self-presence in language, to challenge the authority of origins and subvert the idea that texts necessarily say what they mean, or mean what they say.

Derrida is far from claiming that this exchange represents a 'serious' encounter between two traditions or points of view. In fact his stylistic energies are chiefly directed against the kind of self-approving 'seriousness' which Searle requires of speech-act fidelity in general and philosophic discourse in particular. When Searle refers to 'the suspect status of the "non-serious"', Derrida responds by blithely out-manoeuvring all such protocols of dignity and style. His tactics throughout are a mixture of ingenuous perplexity, mock-rueful bafflement and sheer linguistic cunning. In place of a conclusion Derrida asks himself, 'seriously' enough, whether this strange non-encounter can ever come to an end, or whether indeed it can yet be said to have started.[32]

What is left of my case for seeking out affinities between deconstruction and ordinary-language philosophy? Not much, it might seem, if Derrida's exchange with Searle represented the only possible outcome. But the idea of 'ordinary language' is capable of many interpretations, some of them – like Ryle's – offering a much stronger hold for comparison. Speech-act philosophy as understood by Searle starts out from assumptions so foreign to Derrida's thinking that nothing can result from their encounter save a giddying display of textual ingenuity on Derrida's part. Where Searle rests his case on the sanctions of everyday communicative competence, Derrida exploits the problems created when arguments are pressed against the limits of linguistic possibility. It is Ryle's willingness to *deconstruct* ordinary language – to pursue it into regions of paradox and undecidability – that places him distinctly apart from the normative tradition. I have suggested several reasons for this complex alignment. His early reading of Husserl and Heidegger, along with his unorthodox interest in Plato on the question of writing *versus* speech, are perhaps the most significant pointers in this connection. At the very least his work provides the hint of an alternative to the habit of reciprocal indifference or mistrust which has hitherto prevented any useful exchange between French and Anglo-American philosophers of language. In the following two chapters – on Wittgenstein and Austin – I propose to pursue this alternative into the heartland of modern linguistic philosophy.

2

The insistence of the letter: textuality and metaphor in Wittgenstein's later philosophy

I

A comparison: texts are sometimes hung on the wall. But not theorems of mechanics. (Our relation to these two things.)[1]

Wittgenstein is the authority most often appealed to by those in search of a philosophic case against the claims of deconstruction. For the later Wittgenstein, scepticism could only take hold through the kind of conceptual delinquency which philosophers created when they somehow lost touch with the commonsense bases of ordinary language. The real business of philosophy, he taught, was to coax the mind down from its self-imposed toils of sophisticated questioning and guide it back to a proper sense of linguistic wisdom and health. Philosophic problems were mostly brought about through 'the bewitchment of our intelligence by means of language'.[2] The most effective cure would be to demonstrate that such problems could be made to disappear – or to seem merely marginal and perverse – when restored to a proper linguistic context. The paradigm case for Wittgenstein was that species of radical scepticism, or epistemological doubt, which had long been a major cause of philosophical perplexity. Deconstruction is at present the most rigorous and (to its opponents) the most perverse of all attempts to reckon the consequences of sceptical doubt. It is therefore not surprising that Wittgenstein should be called upon to witness the dangers, the irrelevance, or – as some would have it – the sheer illogicality of deconstructionist thinking.[3]

This chapter takes the view that Wittgenstein's writings by no means provide such a straightforward riposte to the arguments of deconstruction. In fact, as I shall argue, they stand in a distinctly ambivalent relation to those very forms of self-induced sceptical doubt which Wittgenstein professedly chased off limits. This will mean reading Wittgenstein with an eye to such details of figural language as philosophers generally fail to recognize or (more charitably) choose to disregard in the interests of overall consistency and truth. Of course it is widely acknowledged that Wittgenstein's 'style' is closely bound up with his philosophic outlook and characteristic manner of thought. Like Nietzsche (though with very different ends in view) he adopted a cryptic, aphoristic style of address, a mode of perpetual self-interrogation which went along with his rejection of large-scale systematizing philosophy. 'The best that I could write would never be more than philosophical remarks; my thoughts were soon crippled if I tried to force them on in any one direction against their natural inclination.'[4] To this extent, as the commentators agree, Wittgenstein's thought can scarcely be grasped without taking account of his style.

They would probably be less inclined to assent if one pushed this idea to its logical conclusion and argued that philosophic texts should be open to the same techniques of rhetorical close-reading as characterize the more resourceful forms of current literary criticism. Neither should such unwillingness be difficult to understand. The quarrel between philosophy and rhetoric goes back to the beginnings of philosophy's self-image as a higher, truth-telling discipline of thought. Jacques Derrida has set about unearthing the history of 'logocentric' strategies whereby reason has hitherto managed to repress or marginalize the threat of an unbridled figurative language.[5] Philosophy has seen itself as claiming privileged access to a realm of self-sufficient truth which rhetoric (or 'writing', in Derrida's terminology) could only disfigure or distort. Hence the efforts of Locke, among others, to purge his discourse of all metaphorical residues, a project doomed to defeat by the radical metaphoricity of *all* language, not least the sublimated images and figures which philosophy takes for its founding concepts.[6] Hence also the marked devaluation of writing – and the correspondent emphasis on voice, speech and self-presence – which has characterized philosophical discourse from Plato to Husserl and Heidegger.

These are some of the issues and priorities in play when it comes to questioning the figural dimension of philosophic writing. In Wittgenstein's case the defensive symptoms are there to be deciphered in his texts. Metaphor is a major theme in the *Philosophical Investigations*, though one which is often suppressed or occluded when it threatens to surface too insistently. The reason appears to be a problematic tension in Wittgenstein's all-important concept of 'language-games'. This, of course, is the term he applies to all those manifold sense-making habits and conventions which enable language to perform its various legitimate functions in the world. Philosophy is best employed, according to Wittgenstein, in describing these available 'grammars' and showing where language runs into trouble when it 'goes on holiday' or becomes uselessly engrossed in deviant games of its own contriving.

The 'rules' in question must therefore be sufficiently open and flexible to allow for the variety of ways in which language can and does possess intelligible sense. It is no longer a matter – as Wittgenstein had thought when he wrote the *Tractatus* – of analysing ordinary, everyday language into a crystalline structure of logical forms and strict propositional content. 'Logic', 'proposition' and all such specialized concepts can only make sense within the particular language-game that offers a context and criteria for their meaning. The same applies to other, more general notions:

> We see now that what we call 'sentence' and 'language' has not the formal unity that I imagined, but is the family of structures more or less related to one another.... (One might say: the axis of reference of our examination must be rotated, but about the fixed point of our real need.)[7]

On the other hand the 'rules', no matter how varied and provisional, must represent some kind of constitutive limit upon what can be said and understood within a given language-game. The problem with metaphor is that it can, in principle, break with every rule or criterion of fitness which might seem to mark off one game from another, or communicable 'sense' from private 'non-sense'.

Wittgenstein offers a number of examples which manifest his difficulty in dealing with the notion of metaphor. At one point he suggests a distinction between 'primary' and 'secondary' senses of a word, such that the figural (derivative) sense can be treated as somehow integral to the speaker's naturalized expressive repertoire. 'The secondary sense is not a "metaphorical" sense. If I say "For me the vowel *e* is yellow" I do not mean: "yellow" in a metaphorical sense, – for I could not express what I want to say in any other way than by means of the idea "yellow".'[8] But this is surely to entertain the notion of a private language, a stock of associative 'secondary' meanings which could only be fully available to the speaker. It thus contradicts one of Wittgenstein's most basic tenets: that there simply cannot exist a private language capable of making sense outside the intelligible norms and conventions of human exchange. The meaning of words, as he constantly reminds us, is always a function of their *use* in particular (and more or less familiar) contexts. 'If I were to talk to myself out loud in a language not understood by those present my thoughts would be hidden from them'. [9] And again, more vividly: 'If a lion could talk, we could not understand him'.[10] By shifting attention from the problem of metaphor to the notion of 'primary' and 'secondary' meanings, Wittgenstein effectively puts in question his own most basic working metaphor: that of the 'language-game' as source and guarantee of intelligible sense.

Another example may help to focus the problem more sharply. 'Given the two ideas "fat" and "lean", would you be rather inclined to say that Wednesday was fat and Tuesday lean, or *vice versa*?' Wittgenstein inclines toward the former fancy but can offer no rational account for his choice, apart from reflecting that 'they *might* be associations from my childhood'. Yet this, again, seems perilously close to the idea of a private language-game which could not possibly, on Wittgenstein's account, possess any kind of coherent or decidable meaning. The passage goes on: 'Here one might speak of a "primary" and "secondary" sense of a word. It is only if the word has the primary sense for you that you use it in the secondary one.'[11] But how can this distinction be upheld if language itself (as Wittgenstein often implies) is radically metaphorical, based on 'games' of analogy and family-resemblance which cannot be reduced to any single clear-cut logic of representation? It looks very much as though Wittgenstein's awkward dealing with metaphor is indicative of deeper problems and uncertainties in his notion of 'primary' language-games.

II

Deconstruction has to do with precisely such cases of a discourse which represses certain problematic themes (like metaphor) in the interests of preserving its own coherence and authority. Gayatri Spivak describes the deconstructionist project in her Translator's Preface to Derrida's *Of Grammatology*. 'If a metaphor seems to suppress its implications, we shall catch at that metaphor. We shall follow its adventures through the text and see the text coming undone as a structure of concealment, revealing its self-transgression, its undecidability.'[12] In Wittgenstein's case such metaphors are legion and often at odds with what philosophers take as his 'primary' or authentic meaning. Their effect is to complicate the purport of Wittgenstein's arguments with suggestions of an aberrant or excessive figuration beyond intentional control. Indeed, the very concept of 'intention' – a recurrent topic of the text – becomes involved in a chain of metaphorical substitutions where language conspicuously threatens to 'go on holiday'.

The context here is Wittgenstein's discussion of what it means to *speak* or *read* with a full and sensitive awareness of language. We feel that such awareness has to be distinguished from other, less 'responsible' activities, like talking absent-mindedly, just for effect, or 'skimming the page' in search of information. Yet what can this distinction amount to, given Wittgenstein's refusal to entertain arguments from private experience, or from any kind of introspective evidence? He has argued, after all, that meaning is ultimately context-dependent and cannot be grasped, much less analysed, without understanding the language-game involved. This would clearly imply that the 'criteria' for speaking or reading in good earnest are not to be sought in any kind of private, introspective report. And yet: 'When I read a poem or narrative with feeling, surely something goes on in me which does not go on when I merely skim the lines for information'.[13] The problem is to account for that crucial difference without falling prey to the delusion that meaning could ever be a purely private affair, cut off from any validating social context.

Wittgenstein typically pursues the point through a series of extreme examples or limiting cases. What if someone (say a child) were to 'read' a passage which – it then turned out – they had previously learned by heart? Or: what would we say of a subject who, perhaps under the influence of a drug, attached his own sense to a series of arbitrary characters 'with all the outward signs, and with the sensations, of reading?'.[14] Perhaps, suggests Wittgenstein, the difference comes down to our feeling a certain 'influence' exerted on our minds when we genuinely *read* a piece of print. That 'influence' is absent when the putative reader is faced with arbitrary marks on a page, or when he is merely parroting a passage by heart. For practised, fluent readers the exercise is of course artificial; we are normally quite unaware (as Wittgenstein admits) of any such distinguishing influence at work. And this is precisely the kind of self-induced puzzle and strange-seeming 'solution' which philosophy is forced back upon in the face of linguistic 'bewitchment'.

As so often in Wittgenstein's later writing, an answer is no sooner suggested than hedged about with implicit disclaimers and qualifications. This uncertainty is maintained by stylistic devices, especially the use of a shifting and elusive dialogue-form. The different, more-or-less 'authoritative' voices of the text are sometimes distinguished by appearing with or without quotation marks. Elsewhere the pointers are more fugitive, consisting largely of tonal or rhetorical modulations. In the present instance it is hard to be sure just how far Wittgenstein intends to let us go with the idea of reading as marked or distinguished by a sense of some special 'influence' at work on our minds.

Most philosophers would offer a confidently negative reply. We are clearly not meant to accept the idea at anything like face value since it contradicts the basic Wittgensteinian premise: that no such appeal to private, introspectible experience can possibly count as source or guarantee of meaning. This conviction finds support in numerous passages of the *Investigations*. Wittgenstein consistently opposes the view that 'meaning' or 'intention' are ghostly psychological processes which somehow underwrite or serve to authenticate the words which 'express' them. Such a view can only lead to the deluded belief in some 'private language' intelligible on its own special terms and wholly independent of communal usage. This must indeed be Wittgenstein's argument, reading his text as it apparently *means* to be read. But the problem remains if one rejects such a reading and asks instead what questions arise when Wittgenstein's metaphors and speculative parables are really pursued and not held in check by that elusive authorial 'voice'. It is here that deconstruction gets a hold on Wittgenstein's text. And its strategies can hardly be dismissed as perverse, given Wittgenstein's repeated insistence that meanings are embodied in the forms or practices of language, and are not to be sought in private intimations of intent.

A deconstructive reading would bring out the extent to which Wittgenstein depends on *metaphorical* language in striving to negotiate supposedly *conceptual* problems. It might also be expected (following Derrida) that these problems would take on a sharply paradoxical form where philosophy looked for a grounding relation between language, truth and 'authentic' meaning. The thrust of deconstruction is precisely to show that language, in its figural dimension, never permits such a perfectly assured correspondence. Its effect is rather to remove all certainty as to what counts as 'proper' and what as 'figurative' sense. And to cling to this distinction, as Derrida argues, is also to privilege 'voice' (or self-present intention) over the dangerous ambiguities of 'writing'. It should be evident by now that these themes have a close and problematic bearing on Wittgenstein's text. There is, to begin with, the problem of metaphor in relation to 'ordinary language'. There is also the question of 'intentional' meaning and how it can possibly be defined or ascribed to any given piece of language. And these issues converge on the ultimate query as to how far Wittgenstein's authorial intentions are 'there' to be respected, or even understood, as apart from the figural texture of his writing.

The following passage is particularly revealing in the way it both poses and evades its own textual dilemma:

When I pronounce this word while reading with expression it is completely filled with its meaning. – 'How can this be, if meaning is the use of the word?' Well, what I said was intended figuratively. Not that I chose the figure: it forced itself on me. – But the figurative employment of the word can't get into conflict with the original one.[15]

This reasoning is under considerable strain, most of it borne by rhetorical figures and shifts of implication which serve to disguise a deep logical perplexity. The passage starts out by presenting the problem in what seems to be a clearly marked dialogue form. What sense can be attached to the 'expressive' use of language – as opposed to its inert or mechanical utterance – if meaning is wholly identified with 'the use of the word'? Does not the concept of 'language-games' exclude all appeal to a realm of peculiarly *inward* intention somehow distinguishing authentic from merely imitative forms of expression? At this point the dialogue takes a new turn – perhaps a substitution of different 'voices' – explaining that the problem has only come about through the use of figural language. But how did the metaphor ('filled with its meaning') arise in the first place, and how much weight is it intended to bear? If the expression was in any case 'intended figuratively', what can Wittgenstein mean by saying that it was not *chosen* but 'forced itself' upon him? The passage seems unable to resolve its contradictions without producing ever more strained and exiguous twists of metaphorical language. The final sentence can only be seen as a flat refusal to continue this disturbing game. On the face of it the passage demonstrates precisely that figural expressions can and do 'get into conflict' with whatever original or primary sense they are intended to convey.

These symptoms of perplexity only emerge if one resists the deep-seated logocentric assumption that texts embody a communicative power, an authorial 'presence', sufficient to resolve their manifest contradictions. It is by means of this enabling assumption that philosophers can extract from Wittgenstein a plausibly coherent account of his ideas about meaning and language. And indeed, his style does much to encourage this response, with its suasive deployment of tonal variations and oblique, dialogical shifts of viewpoint, all of which work strongly to imply a commanding authorial strategy behind them. The reader is understandably tempted to accept the idea of an animating 'presence' which seems to guarantee the significance and purport of Wittgenstein's intended meaning. Language is saved from its own most dangerous (textual) devices by this sense of an authenticating purpose at work. 'Every sign *by itself* seems dead. *What* gives it life? – In use it is *alive*. Is life breathed into it there? – Or is the *use* its life?'[16] This passage must of course be read as subject to the qualifying doubts and ironies which always mark Wittgenstein's dealing with subjectivist ideas. Yet it plays too significant a role in his argument simply to be written off as a passing fancy or speculative fiction. Might it not be the case that Wittgenstein's text is interpretable *only* if its language affords access to some such realm of authentic intent?

It would seem, therefore, that a reading of the *Philosophical Investigations* must proceed along one or the other of two very different paths. The 'standard' interpretation would take it for granted that texts normally say what they mean and mean what they say, except perhaps in marginal cases where language momentarily 'goes on holiday'. Such instances call for corrective treatment – Wittgenstein's notion of philosophy as a kind of therapeutic exercise – and therefore serve only to confirm the general rule. In a healthy state of language the mind is not troubled by those specialized, misguided questionings which vex traditional philosophy. It is only when thought becomes obsessed with its own workings – when 'the engine is idling', to borrow Wittgenstein's metaphor – that problems arise which seem to demand 'philosophical' answers. Otherwise it simply does not make sense to ask (for instance) what relationship exists between meaning and intention, or expression and the language-game within which meaning finds utterance. Such might be termed the 'primary' reading of the *Philosophical Investigations*, using that word (as Wittgenstein uses it) to marginalize or contain the effects of a 'secondary' reading which might interfere with his argumentative purpose. Primary understanding is in this sense the normative discourse of philosophy at large. It involves what Derrida would seek to reveal as the logocentric closure, or covert 'metaphysics of presence', where meaning and truth are assumed to coincide in a self-sufficient state of original linguistic grace.

Such, in broad outline, is one – and by now the traditional – way of interpreting Wittgenstein's text. The other, let us say 'deconstructionist' reading, is of the kind this chapter has begun to broach. It refuses to accept on trust those powerful normative conventions (of coherence, authority, 'primary' meaning) which govern most interpretation. Likewise, it rejects the idea that figurative language necessarily takes rise from a primary, literal sense which is philosophy's proper concern. It is alert, above all, to those metaphors of voice and self-presence which would seem to act as a defensive brake upon the otherwise threatening play of linguistic figuration. A deconstructionist would claim that her reading was scrupulously close to the letter, if not the 'spirit', of Wittgenstein's text. She might also remark – with a good show of evidence – that the text offers grounds of its own for doubting whether any such 'spirit', however conceived, should properly influence its interpretation. This would simply mean pointing to Wittgenstein's rejection of mentalist imagery and his refusal to assimilate meaning to psychological or subjective mind-states. In short, the deconstructionist might claim that philosophers – especially professing Wittgensteinians – had not yet got round to *reading* Wittgenstein's text with anything like an adequately detailed attention.

At one point Wittgenstein calls language a 'labyrinth of paths'. In his own text the tracks of meaning and metaphor constantly cross and redouble until it seems that no firm sense can be attached to some of his major terms. 'You approach from *one* side and know your way about; you approach the same place from another side and no longer know your way about'.[17] Ordinary-language philosophy would have us believe that this condition is a local and specialized 'bewitchment' curable by means of restoring language to its natural or proper context. Along with this conviction goes the general belief that a line can be drawn between legitimate, primary usage and those deviant forms, whatever their nature – misguided or merely 'metaphorical' – which somehow transgress the norm. Deconstruction challenges each of these premises and carries its challenge as far as possible into the texts which ostensibly support them. Metaphor is not an incidental supplement to literal or 'primary' meaning. Rather, it pervades the very texture of language in so many forms (whether overt or disguised) that its effects are not to be contained by philosophical fiat. These effects are always liable – as Derrida shows – to disrupt or disfigure any notional priority of 'origin' to 'supplement', 'speech' to 'writing' or literal sense to figural detour. And Wittgenstein's text is highly susceptible to deconstruction, despite all the signs that its 'primary' or manifest intent is to render such sceptical philosophies simply unthinkable.

III

The most insistent metaphors in the *Investigations* are those which stand in for a vaguely defined notion of intentionality. We have seen already how Wittgenstein distinguishes 'lifeless', routine or merely imitative uses of language from those which convey the vitalizing presence of expressive intent. Signs are otherwise 'dead' or inert, mere inscriptions on the page which might as well be random figurations or elements of an alien, arbitrary code. What Wittgenstein is hinting at here is a form of phenomenological appeal to the process of *reading* as a type or test-case of meaningful (intentional) activity. And around this theme there emerges a cluster of related topics and images which foreground the question of *writing* (or print) as a somehow disquieting phenomenon.

Derrida has shown the extent to which writing has always been repressed or devalued in the western metaphysical tradition.[18] Writing is viewed as 'parasitical' on speech, a secondary medium of arbitrary signs deprived of the authenticating 'presence' vested in spoken language. In various symptomaticforms – from Plato's *Phaedrus* to Saussurean linguistics or the Rousseauist nostalgia of Lévi-Strauss – writing is represented as a fall from grace, a 'dangerous supplement' threatening the pristine self-presence of speech. 'The letter killeth; the spirit giveth life.' At best, writing is the faithful transcription of a primary spoken truth. At worst, it is the source of boundless duplicity and error, the fate in store for language when wrenched from the authentic context of voice and communicative presence.

A similar fear seems to haunt Wittgenstein's arguments, though never explicitly acknowledged as such. What if language were 'arbitrary' through and through, and not just in those deviant or marginal cases which Wittgenstein examines? How would things stand for philosophy if the 'breath' or 'life' of meaning were indeed a species of enabling illusion, presupposed in all our dealings with language but none the less illusory for that? Wittgenstein's case against 'private' language-games and mentalist criteria forces him at least to entertain this disturbing possibility. 'I said that when one reads the spoken words come "in a special way": but in what way? Isn't this a fiction?'.[19] No answer is forthcoming, but rather a series of therapeutic moves and counter-moves designed to relieve the craving for solutions where no real problem exists. 'Remember that the look of a word is familiar to us in the same kind of way as its sound'.[20] The sense of disquiet induced by writing can be kept at bay so long as the inscription is treated as a strictly secondary adjunct to *speech*. Only by assimilating written language to a form of inward *vocal* enactment can Wittgenstein quell his recurrent feelings of unease. Textuality can thus be redeemed from the condition of 'lifeless' arbitrary signs and restored to the community of intersubjective meaning.

This enables the reader to experience once again 'the familiar physiognomy of a word, the feeling that it has taken up its meaning into itself, that it is an actual likeness of its meaning'.[21] Yet might there not exist, Wittgenstein then asks, 'human beings to whom all this was alien? (They would not have an attachment to their words.)' It is a query which can neither be answered nor lightly dismissed. It serves rather to beat the bounds of that proper, intelligible language-game which Wittgenstein wishes to set in its place. Once recognize the pointlessness of raising such questions and they might just disappear into the limbo of misguided philosophical talk whence they arose in the first place. But if this is the intended drift of Wittgenstein's reasoning – and the message expounded by his faithful commentators – it is still not capable of dispelling the doubts which periodically assail his text. There remains a constant undertow of figural suggestion which naggingly pulls against any firm assurance of the power to distinguish between 'live' (meaningful) and 'dead' (arbitrary) language-games.

This problem is rendered all the more acute because Wittgenstein clings to his phonocentric metaphors of writing and reading as derivative forms of *speech*. What is in question is not merely the obvious fact that each written language employs certain standard graphic conventions by way of representing sequences of phonetic material. Such would be the case by definition with any alphabetical–phonetic script. Rather, it is the way in which Wittgenstein uses the privileged *metaphors* of voice and speech to insinuate the claim of authentic (self-present) intelligibility as opposed to the empty figurations of an alien writing. Without this analogy, it seems, meaningful language would be simply indistinguishable from all the varieties of arbitrary code and random unintelligible gesture.

Wittgenstein's metaphors are structured by the same systematic priority of 'speech' over 'writing' that Derrida traces down through the history of western philosophic tradition. In Derrida's words: 'the philosophical text, although it is in fact always written, includes, precisely as its philosophical specificity, the project of effacing itself in the face of the signified content which it transports and in general teaches.'[22] This priority of the signified in turn leads back to a putative grounding in speech and self-presence, a gesture that identifies consciousness itself with the absolute privilege granted to vocal expression. 'Such is at least the experience – or consciousness – of the voice: of hearing (understanding) oneself-speak (*s'entendre-parler*).'[23] And the ethos of speech as self-presence entails a correspondingly negative attitude to written language. 'That experience lives and proclaims itself as the exclusion of writing, that is to say of the invoking of an "exterior", "sensible", "spatial" signifier interrupting self-presence.'[24]

If Derrida sets out to deconstruct this tradition of phonocentric thinking, Wittgenstein perpetually comes up against its limits from within. This contrast may indeed be overstated, since Derrida himself acknowledges that thought can never achieve a standpoint 'outside' the metaphysical assumptions which permeate all language, his own included. At best it can maintain a vigilant awareness of the metaphors and pre-critical motives which everywhere threaten to deflect the work of deconstruction. Wittgenstein has a passage to similar effect in the context of discussing his earlier (*Tractatus*) ideal of a perfectly articulated logical language, purged of natural ambiguity:

> The ideal, as we think of it, is unshakable. You can never get outside it; you must always turn back. There is no outside; outside you cannot breathe. – Where does this idea come

from? It is like a pair of glasses on our nose through which we see whatever we look at. It never occurs to us to take them off.[25]

It is clearly implicit that we *can* and *should* remove the spectacles, simply by renouncing (along with Wittgenstein) the false picture of language and logic which previously held us captive. But where does this renunciation lead? In Wittgenstein's case, to a notion of language that exchanges one kind of philosophic closure for another, less rigorously limiting but equally problematic in its textual effects.

The most obvious of these is the dualist implication that 'outward' activities (such as writing, or going through the motions of reading) must somehow be accompanied by an answering 'inward' process. Wittgenstein is expressly at pains to reject this idea, and his attempts have been seconded by those (like Gilbert Ryle) who have sought to demolish the entire Cartesian myth of 'the ghost in the machine'.[26] Such is the intended significance of Wittgenstein's repudiating private or mentalist criteria of meaning in favour of the broadly consensual basis provided by the idiom of 'language-games'. But the dualist metaphors persist, questioned but by no means exorcised in a passage like the following:

> Silent 'internal' speech is not a half-hidden phenomenon which is as it were seen through a veil. It is not hidden *at all*, but the concept may easily confuse us, for it runs over a long stretch cheek by jowl with the concept of an 'outward' process, and yet does not coincide with it.[27]

The reader is implicitly warned against accepting *certain* problematic metaphors – those of 'hiddenness' and private experience – which would throw an obvious paradox into Wittgenstein's philosophy. On the other hand his description clings to the idea of 'silent "internal" speech', even while suggesting (by its use of those typical quotation marks) that the phrase is not to be taken at face value.

The effects of deconstruction are already at work in these twists and contestations of Wittgenstein's text. He is attempting to articulate a crucial distinction which can only be presented in figural guise, yet which seems to be double-crossed or undermined at every stage by his very choice of metaphorical terms. Derrida's deconstructive reading of Husserl offers a close and revealing parallel here.[28] Husserl sets out to establish phenomenology through an absolute grounding in reflective self-evidence embodied in the forms of thought and language. This involves the process of 'phenomenological reduction', a self-imposed critique of consciousness and mental representation whereby the essential structures of mind are distinguished from their empirical or psychological content. Only thus, according to Husserl, can the 'crisis of reason' be squarely confronted and philosophy restored to a confidence in truth and the power of language to encompass and express it.[29] Reason is guaranteed on the one hand by an assurance that its forms of linguistic representation correspond to the structures of reality (time and space) presented to human understanding. On the other, it finds an authentic *subjective* grounding in the link between language and intentionality, significant expression and the correlated structures of meaningful inward awareness.

Derrida typically fastens on the logocentric premises which underlie and govern Husserl's entire project. He points out the metaphors of voice as self-presence, the equation between genuine, authentic sense and the image of a consciousness pictured as ideally coinciding with its own expressive intent. In Derrida's reading, this equation structures each and every move by which Husserl attempts to validate the findings of phenomenological enquiry. Language, truth and logic are all construed as finally dependent on a validating content of intentional activity identified with pure self-presence. And along with this priority there appears, once again, that constant relegation of *writing* – or merely graphic conventions – to a realm of lifeless, mechanical signification. Husserl, like Wittgenstein, articulates this difference through a series of supposedly self-evident contrasts and exclusions. Most important – for Husserl and for Derrida's reading – is the cardinal distinction between 'expressive' and 'indicative' signs. The former are conceived as bearers of a self-present meaningful intention which serves to authenticate their manifest sense. The latter are devoid of this expressive potential, existing merely as empty signs or arbitrary tokens of a purely conventional character. Husserl is obliged to maintain this distinction in view of his phenomenological appeal to intentionality as source and gurantee of meaning.

Derrida shows, with exemplary precision, the extent to which Husserl's arguments founder on conceptual problems of their own (logocentric) creating. His texts not only fail to preserve the distinction between 'expressive' and 'indicative' signs, but point to the conclusion that language can *only* be conceived in terms of an arbitrary signifying network devoid of all original expressive intent. Language is always already caught up in structures of convention or pre-existent sense which effectively bar any appeal to self-present intention as the locus of meaning. Communication is only possible, indeed, by virtue of the fact that language can be detached from its original expressive intent and still possess meaning as part of the generalized economy of signs. Husserl conceives language on the model of face-to-face communicative utterance, an extension of the metaphor which privileges inward speech above the detours and vagaries of writing. And moreover, as Derrida goes on to show, writing is coextensive with the realm of 'indicative' signs which pose such a threat to Husserl's undertaking. On the one side speech bears its traditional connotations of life-giving presence, naturalness and immediacy. On the other stands writing with its associated properties of absence, difference, exteriority and arbitrary signification. What Derrida brings out most strikingly is the extent to which images of writing – or the functions of 'indicative' language – invade the grounding metaphors of Husserlian phenomenology.

The following passage from Derrida will help both to focus his critique of Husserl and to point up its relevance to our reading of Wittgenstein. It is evident, Derrida writes:

> that this *de facto* necessity of entanglement, intimately associating expression and indication, must not, according to Husserl, cut off the possibility of a rigorous distinction of essence. This possibility is purely *de jure* and phenomenological. The whole analysis will thus advance in this separation between *de facto* and *de jure*, existence and essence, reality and intentional function. . . . This separation does not exist prior to the question of language . . . its *de jure* import depends entirely on language and, in language, on the validity of a radical distinction between indication and expression.[30]

The *de facto* necessity that Derrida invokes is the order of meaning forced upon Husserl's text by a logic seemingly outside its intentional control. The *de jure* project of phenomenological reduction is wrenched from its original purpose by the effects of this aberrant (but strictly consequential) logic. It thus becomes impossible to take full measure of Husserl's arguments without becoming conscious of a radical divergence between intention and meaning, voice and text, authorial presence and the effects of writing.

IV

We have already seen something of this disjunctive textual logic as it affects Wittgenstein's later philosophy. Problems about language – however illusory Wittgenstein considers them – are focused most sharply on the instances of *writing* and *reading*. These raise the question of what 'goes on' when we engage with language in a fully attentive and responsive way. They also suggest, more disturbingly, that no real sense can be attached to this question; that what 'goes on' cannot be accounted for otherwise than by figural descriptions, themselves equally (or more) problematical. This dilemma produces two opposed strains of metaphor. On the one hand they work to assimilate writing and reading to a phonocentric notion of 'inward speech' which inevitably tends to imply – despite Wittgenstein's repeated disclaimers – that meaning is some kind of private, introspectible process. On the other hand they issue in the form of those insistently *graphic* examples and reminders which punctuate Wittgenstein's text. It is as if the sheer materiality of writing constantly obtruded itself by way of resisting the phonocentric bias of his thought.

This insistence of the letter is felt most keenly in those passages where Wittgenstein attempts to describe the deep *familiarity* or preconscious naturalness of our usual reading experience. Normally, written or printed language has a 'special appearance', a consistency of graphic aspect and sequence which affects us very differently from 'arbitrary' marks on a page. Most of the words we encounter in reading are 'constantly repeated and enormously familiar to us, like well-known faces'.[31] And to make his point more forcefully, Wittgenstein asks us to think of 'the uneasiness we feel when the spelling of a word is changed. (And of the still stronger feelings that questions about the spelling of words have aroused)'.[32] This reflection is intended to strengthen our sense of the natural, 'familiar' quality which somehow attends our normal activity of reading. At the same time, however, it has to admit the disruptive effect of changes in spelling, changes that cannot (after all) be seen as departing from any natural or 'proper' system of representation. Spelling is largely a matter of convention, no less so when it happens to accord with our normal writing and reading experience. Whatever 'deep feelings' may be aroused by deviant or anomalous spelling, they can only have to do with arbitrary rules which in principle admit of no appeal to natural usage.

All this may seem obvious enough. Yet Wittgenstein implies, by his use of this example, that there *must* be some intuitively graspable distinction between standard and deviant spelling. He asks us to believe that the exception proves the rule; that 'arbitrary' changes make us more aware of the otherwise smoothly unimpeded process of assimilating print. Yet his argument lies open to another interpretation, one which would see the exception as *pre-empting* any possible 'rule'. If graphic notation is in any case governed by a wholly conventional system of signs, then clearly its workings are always and everywhere 'arbitrary', and not just those instances which strikingly break with accepted convention. And this suggests in turn that language may be subject to a *generalized* arbitrariness, the effects of which are most clearly visible where writing resists its own customary effacement in the service of a self-present 'inward' speech.

There are several passages in the *Investigations* which register a sense of this unsettling possibility. If the relation between language-games and the meanings they convey is aptly figured in the processes of writing and reading, then any suggestion of an *arbitrary* linkage at this point must strike at the heart of Wittgenstein's philosophy. Such is precisely the problem engendered by his constantly reverting to the instances of script and print. The following passage underlines this paradox:

> I can imagine some arbitrary cipher [Wittgenstein provides an example] to be a strictly correct letter of some foreign

alphabet. Or again, to be a faultily written one, and faulty in this way or that: for example, it might be slap-dash, or typical childish awkwardness, or like the flourishes in a legal document. It could deviate from the correctly written letter in a variety of ways. – And I can see it in various aspects according to the fiction I surround it with. And here there is a close kinship with 'experiencing the sense of a word'.[33]

The reasoning here has paradoxical consequences for Wittgenstein's philosophy of language. It is markedly at odds with the distinction he attempts to draw elsewhere between genuine (meaningful) and merely 'arbitrary' signs. The random cipher is taken up into an equally random language-game of private-associative meanings. This provides the cipher with some kind of familiarizing context, and the reader with a means to assimilate its 'foreign' or otherwise perplexing character. That Wittgenstein goes on to compare such arbitrary 'fictions' with the business of 'experiencing the meaning of a word' can only be seen as strangely out of keeping with his general views. What is left to distinguish such 'deviant' signs from the naturalized conventions and language-games of 'normal' communicative discourse?

It is a similar logic which Derrida sees at work in the undoing of Husserlian phenomenology. The privilege attaching to 'expressive' language is deconstructed by the constant intrusion of 'indicative' signs and tokens, products of a differential signifying network where meaning never coincides with pure, self-present intentionality. The twin ideas of 'differing' and 'deferring' are both played upon in Derrida's punning key-term *differance*.[34] As deployed in his reading of Husserl it signifies, firstly, that play of illimitable 'difference' within language which operates to disturb or prevent any conceivable relation of self-present identity between signifier and signified. Secondly, it suggests that process of *temporal* displacement which intervenes when Husserl (in *The Phenomenology of Internal Time-Consciousness*) attempts to isolate a moment of present experience in which traces of memory and anticipation are fully subsumed. Husserl's logocentric premises are subject to a constant differential or temporalizing movement – a 'spacing' within language and consciousness – which offers itself to deconstructive reading.

Consider the role of 'difference' in the following passage from Wittgenstein:

> It would never have occurred to us to think that we *felt the influence* of the letters on us when reading, if we had not compared the case of letters with that of arbitrary marks. And here we are indeed noticing a *difference*. And we interpret it as the difference between being influenced and not being influenced.[35]

Wittgenstein is implicitly rejecting this idea of a ghostly 'influence' exerted by language when we read with plenary understanding. The 'difference' in question would thus seem illusory, the outcome of a misleading metaphor. Yet Wittgenstein appears unwilling or unable to let go of it entirely. The passage goes on to suggest that the 'influence-idea occurs to us most readily 'when we make a point of reading slowly – perhaps in order to see what does happen when we read. When we, so to speak, quite intentionally let ourselves be guided by the letters'.[36] Again, this notion is immediately placed in doubt: the idea of 'letting myself be guided' can only consist in my 'looking carefully at the letters' and perhaps in deliberately 'excluding certain other thoughts'. What we read in this passge is the shuttling movement between phonocentric metaphors and a purely *inscriptional* account – 'looking carefully at the letters' – which is all that Wittgenstein can offer by way of corrective emphasis. The 'difference' which Wittgenstein suggestively invokes – only to cancel the suggestion straight away – is deeply inscribed in the logic of his argument.

Here, as in Husserl, the theme of 'lived' or expressive language is everywhere shadowed by what seems an almost involuntary recourse to images of 'lifeless' script or print. Wittgenstein is left with no choice but to alternate between metaphors of ghostly 'influence' and a blank phenomenology of reading which reduces to simply 'looking carefully at the letters'. This in turn represents the predicament of a philosophy waylaid by textual turns of metaphor which it can neither acknowledge nor fully expunge from its writing. In Wittgenstein's text, the recourse to phonocentric imagery sometimes produces an almost Cratylist persuasion that the graphic and phonetic qualities of words are somehow intimately linked to their meaning:

Thus I might say that the written word *intimates* the sound to me. – Or again, that when one reads, letter and sound form a *unity* – as it were an alloy. (In the same way e.g. the faces of famous men and the sound of their names are fused together. This name strikes me as the only right one for this face.)[37]

As usual the image is swiftly disclaimed, put down to the persistence of a mental 'picture' which fails to represent our normal experience of reading. But the picture retains a powerful hold on Wittgenstein's thought, revived whenever he puts forward the crucial idea of meaning as 'aspect' or 'seeing-as'. If our grasping the sense of a word is akin to the dawning of its proper 'aspect', then there must indeed exist some intimate link between sound, letter and meaning. Such metaphors bear too much weight in Wittgenstein's text simply to be dismissed as passing illustrative fancies.

What is the significance, for example, of his choosing the image of an *alloy* (in the passage quoted above) to suggest that sense of an inward bond between sound, meaning and graphic representation? (Anscombe's rendering of the German *Legierung* by 'alloy' is sufficiently literal and unproblematic to justify such close attention.) With his early training and lifelong interest in matters mechanical, Wittgenstein is unlikely to have used the word with just a casual sense of its metaphoric overtones. And these, if one pursues them, open up a range of conflicting possibilities which have a distinct bearing on the passage in question.

The *Oxford English Dictionary* provides evidence of a complex semantic history for the word 'alloy'. At its most straightforward the meaning is given as: 'the condition of a combination between different metals melted together.' More often, however, it seems to have been used with connotations of relative dignity or worth; thus 'admixture of that which lowers the character or takes from the value'. But the process also worked in the opposite direction, as explained by the following etymological note:

Through the erroneous fancy that French *aloi* was = à loi 'to law', the word, meaning originally simple 'combination', 'union', came to be used specifically of the mixing of a baser metal with gold or silver in coinage, so as to bring it to the recognized standard, and hence of the standard itself.

This ambivalence is carried over into figurative uses of the word. Since it also brings out a distinct double aspect to the *physical* process involved, its paradoxical implications are likely to be that much more insistent.

But why attach such a weight of significance to Wittgenstein's isolated metaphor? Firstly, because it figures at a stage in his argument where certain tensions have developed, tensions which are focused and (at least for the moment) resolved through Wittgenstein's hitting on this image. Secondly, because it offers a compact example of how figurative language works both to advance and to complicate the argument in hand. The 'alloy' of inscription, sound and sense is apparently conceived as a balanced, harmonious unity, a non-evaluative 'mixture and combination' as the dictionary defines it. On the other hand the metaphor also picks up something of the complex, contradictory, prejudicial strain which marks Wittgenstein's various encounters with the problematic instance of writing. Of course it is strictly undecidable which, if either, is the 'baser' element, sound or inscription; or whether indeed the resultant alloy is of a higher or lower value than the notional 'standard'. The standard itself (as the *OED* suggests) can only be defined in relation to the changeable and arbitrary mixture which composes the coinage. In the same way meaning, as Wittgenstein conceives it, appears indescribable except by recourse to the highly unstable 'union' of sound and script. The 'alloy' metaphor thus comes to stand as a peculiarly pregnant example of the effects, within philosophy, of metaphor and writing in general. Its evaluative ambiguities – levelling up or levelling down according to an arbitrary currency – suggest most aptly the textual predicament of Wittgenstein's creating.

V

Of course such a reading goes far beyond what most philosophers would regard as the limits of responsible interpretation. It tends to be assumed, once a text achieves canonical status, that the business of commentary is to seek out coherence and intelligibility, to justify the text on its own argumentative terms. Behind this general consensus is the even more basic presupposition: that writing is always in principle subordinate to the meaning, intention or generalized argument it serves to convey. That texts might not always say what they mean, or that figural language (in Wittgenstein's words) might 'get in the way' of its primary sense, are marginal possibilities which philosophers mostly prefer not to consider. Still less can they entertain the monstrous idea that the discourse of philosophy is everywhere subject to a play of rhetorical signification which exceeds all the bounds of intentional restraint.

Such is the lesson that Derrida reads in Plato's *Phaedrus*, a text which allegorizes the dangers of writing and the need to protect both speech and philosophy against its insidious, subversive effects.[38] Derrida's reading might well be called 'masterly', were it not for the insistence that writing can *never* be mastered, never harnessed to a privileged order of sense, whether by authorial intent or interpretative will. Plato's metaphors are shown to hinge on a series of uncanny ambiguities. Writing is both denounced (as a poison, a parasite, a 'dead' mnemotechnic device) and at the same time shown to be everywhere at work within language, even – if one pursues Plato's metaphors – at the heart of speech and truth. The reader is confronted with a strange double logic which defies all normal (philosophic) reason and belongs to the order of *textual* inscription, where alone its multiple meanings can be kept in play. The most notable ambiguity is that of the *pharmakon*, which can signify both 'poison' and 'cure'. As Derrida describes it:

> The word *pharmakon* is caught in a chain of significations. The play of that chain seems systematic. But the system here is not, simply, that of the intentions of an author who goes by the name of Plato. The system is not primarily that of what someone *meant-to-say* (*un vouloir-dire*). Finely regulated communications can be established, through the play of language . . . these corridors of meaning can sometimes be declared or clarified by Plato when he plays upon them 'voluntarily', a word we put in quotation marks because what it designates . . . is only a mode of 'submission' to the necessities of a given 'language'.[39]

I have quoted this passage at length because it bears directly on those questions of writing and figural signification which emerge through a deconstructive reading of Wittgenstein's text. There also we can witness what Derrida calls the 'disseminating' influence of writing, its power to unfix and unsettle the self-possessed concepts of philosophic reason.

This would mean attending to Wittgenstein's metaphors, not merely as illustrative pointers, no sooner used than dispensed with, but as playing a decisive (though perhaps *undecidable*) role in his text. This approach can hardly be described as perverse, given the sheer number of exemplary 'cases' which Wittgenstein expressly uses for the sake of their oblique or metaphorical significance. What is in question is a reading that takes him consistently *at his word*, rather than assenting to the flat denial that such figurative meanings can 'get in the way' of some ulterior, primary import. It then becomes clear that metaphors of writing and textuality exert a constant hold on Wittgenstein's thought, a power of suggestion that generates both its characteristic insights and its moments of equally characteristic blindness.

One last example may serve to demonstrate how even an apparently casual metaphor can enter this complex weave of figural associations. Wittgenstein is arguing against the idea that reflections on the nature and limits of philosophy belong to a separate level of discourse, a 'metaphilosophical' order of enquiry:

> One might think: if philosophy speaks of the use of the word 'philosophy' there must be a second-order philosophy. But it is not so: it is, rather, like the case of orthography, which deals with the word 'orthography' among others without then being second-order.[40]

This analogy is more complex than might at first appear. It involves a double logic of comparison, on the one hand moving from orthography (spelling) to the idea of philosophy at large, and on the other from the spelling of 'orthography' itself to philosophy as it tries to comprehend its own proper scope. The intended point is that philosophic discourse *always* includes such reflexive implications, so that really there is no sense in talking about 'second-order' philosophy. In the same way, orthography can treat of the spelling of its own name – as one particular case among many – without for that reason suddenly shifting to a different, higher level of discourse.

But does the analogy really take effect as Wittgenstein seems to intend? Can philosophy relate to its own investigations in the same purely arbitrary way as 'orthography' (or the spelling thereof) to the science it denotes? On the face of it this would imply that philosophy is not so much a unified activity as a field in which random encounters occur between first-order topics and the second-order discourse that tries to comprehend them. In fact what the analogy suggests – contrary to Wittgenstein's intention – is something more akin to his idea in the *Tractatus* of a logical meta-language exempt from the confusions of fact and value created by ordinary usage. Once again, it is the image of a literal *writing* which enters to perturb the drift of Wittgenstein's argument, in this case reducing philosophical reflection to a 'second-order' science of arbitrary signs.

'A simile that has been absorbed into the forms of our language produces a false appearance, and this disquiets us. "But *this* is not how it is!" – we say. "Yet *this* is how it has to be" '.[41] Such similes, pressed to the limits of sense, are Wittgenstein's most powerful aids in curing the 'bewitchment' of intelligence by language. No philosopher has been more aware of the mazy confusions engendered by certain kinds of metaphor embedded in our habits of thought. But Wittgenstein's text also bears the marks of another, more pervasive form of bewitchment: the effects of textuality itself as alternately revealed and repressed in philosophic writing. That these effects are not peculiar to Wittgenstein's writing becomes evident – as I now go on to argue – if one examines the case of J. L. Austin and speech-act philosophy.

3

'That the truest philosophy is the most feigning': Austin on the margins of literature

J. L. Austin appears to have shared with Socrates – or at least, with Plato's version of Socrates – a conviction that writing was in some sense inimical to the proper pursuit of philosophic wisdom. His published texts are small in bulk and certainly far outweighed by the volume of secondary writing which has built up around them. Furthermore, they are couched for the most part in a style of offhand, colloquial observation which works to suggest a much larger background of tacit knowledge than writing – mere writing – can hope to comprehend. Among the commentators there is a widespread agreement that Austin's texts come nowhere near conveying the authority, power and inspirational quality of his first-hand teaching and seminar talk. Roderick Firth echoes many of them when he writes: 'It is unlikely that the philosophical genius of the late John Austin will ever be adequately appreciated by those who have merely read his words in print.'[1] Nor, apparently, is there much hope of enlightenment for those who were privileged only to attend Austin's lectures. 'Brilliant' though these sometimes were, to listen to them could only be a matter of feeling remote 'reverberations' of the analytic genius which left such a mark on his immediate disciples. J. O. Urmson (Austin's literary executor) likewise takes it for granted that his was 'a method of discovery and not of presentation', such that the essential import of his procedures 'could not be followed in writings'.[2]

No doubt such cliquishness is common enough among followers of a dead master, one whose wisdom is entrusted to their keeping and is threatened, they feel, by the fact that his texts are available to all kinds of delinquent misinterpretation. But in Austin's case one may hazard the guess that there are motivating factors more intimately linked to the character of his thinking and the nature of its influence. Austin, after all, was pre-eminently the founder of speech-act philosophy, a technique or outlook which attached great significance to the kinds of communal, tacit understanding which underlie the surface workings of language. Written texts may partake of this condition; indeed, they *must* so partake (Austin would argue) if we are ever to construe their meaning in anything like a faithful, undistorted sense. Yet the fact of their existing only in written form – deprived of the animating presence, the authentic give-and-take of spoken discourse – places them apparently at one remove from genuine philosophic truth. Like Plato on Socrates, Austin's disciples are condemned to rehearse *in writing* a philosophy which would, if possible, dispense with such a compromised means of transmission and practise its powers upon a small, select company of like-minded auditors. Hence the frequent reference to those famous 'Saturday mornings' in Oxford when Austin could perform to the top of his bent without fear of rivalry or misinterpretation.

But what of the *texts* which must – for better or worse – survive as the best means of access to Austin's thought for readers outside that privileged but mortal community? Are we entitled to assume – again like Plato – that the inherent liabilities of writing can be held within bounds by a faithful devotion to the truth handed down from its author to those wise enough to grasp it? In terms of speech-act philosophy these questions are capable of sharper formulation. How far is our reading of texts constrained by those kinds of 'illocutionary force', or performative intent, which Austin eventually came to regard not just as a special case but as the virtual precondition of language? The issue comes down to a matter of interpretative ethics, of asking what consequences follow from the fact that we are *reading* Austin, rather than passing on our privileged first-hand impression of what he 'really' thought or meant. Do Austin's own texts bear out their claim by exhibiting a consistency of argument and ethos which would make it impossible – except by a perverse misreading – to mistake their intentional import? Austin's ideas were notoriously subject to constant visions and revisions. But the burden of his arguments was always such as to place a peculiar stress on this question of *how* – by what special claims of good faith and proper understanding – we can actually believe (if we do) that language means what it says and says what it means. No amount of vague talk about Austin's personal authority will suffice to clinch the case for a 'true' (i.e. a faithfully Austinian) reading of his texts. Any problems with interpreting their sense, intention or details of argument will throw a very sizeable paradox into the whole philosophy of meaningful utterance associated with Austin's name.

Derrida, for one, has seized upon precisely such textual symptoms of ambivalence and strain.[3] Derrida's argument strikes at the basis of speech-act philosophy by systematically disregarding the privileged status of spoken language. Austin himself makes much of the point that his various 'performatives' are largely dependent on types of linguistic *convention* – codes and protocols of discourse – without which their force would go unrecognized. 'I pronounce you man and wife' is an act which presupposes both a proper (institutionally approved) form of words and a whole complex set of legitimating circumstances whereby the ceremony is ratified. Austin would argue that genuine (or 'felicitous') speech-acts must also involve a present good faith on the speaker's part, an understanding that his or her words are sincerely meant and not simply uttered as a matter of empty convention. A performative utterance, Austin writes, will be *'in a peculiar way* hollow or void if said by an actor on the stage, or if introduced in a poem, or spoken in soliloquy'.[4] Derrida's deconstructive strategy is to pick out these supposedly marginal examples and ask by what absolute philosophic *right* they are excluded as mere aberrations. If speech-acts are conventional, 'iterable' forms of language – defined, that is, by the fact that they can be repeated word for word in various contexts, but with the same operative 'force' – then how can Austin think to distinguish genuine from merely 'hollow' or 'void' varieties? Performatives are always already inscribed in a play of linguistic convention which works to undermine any clear-cut notion of authentic intent.

For Derrida, there is a further point of interest (or deconstructive leverage) in the fact that Austin has to exclude such 'literary' uses of language as poetry, dramatic dialogue or any kind of fictional discourse. This goes along with his need to draw a line between authentic speech-acts and cases where the same verbal formula is merely *cited* or offered by way of second-hand exemplification. Such instances, for Austin, can only be regarded as 'parasitic' or 'etiolated' speech-acts, a move which effectively prevents them from creating any serious trouble when he comes to consider the genuine article. But what if these deviant cases were in fact – as Derrida argues – not deviant at all but part and parcel of the 'iterability' which marks all performatives, spoken or written? This would imply that the conventional nature of speech-acts *in general* is such as to bar any firm distinction between those uttered in present good faith – 'serious' instances as Austin terms them – and those which possess only a token, citational or 'parasitic' sense. It would thus present an obstacle to Austin's belief that performatives, properly so called, are not just a matter of obeying some empty convention but involve a special commitment on the speaker's part. The whole terminology of speech-act theory reveals, in Derrida's reading, an attachment to the ethos of voice-as-presence, the assumption that there exists some intimate link between speech and that inward, immediate consciousness of meaning which makes for genuine expression. The obverse of this belief is the unease which shows itself in Austin's handling of written (or literary) forms of language. Texts are always open to diverse interpretations, deprived as they are of the face-to-face presence, the communicative closeness of speech situations. Writing is prey to all those dangerous derivative instances which threaten the integrity of speech and speech-act theory alike.

This suggests that there is more than traditional piety involved when Austin's disciples repeatedly stress the inadequacy of his *writings* to convey any notion of the wisdom and profundity of his *talk*. The privilege accorded to speech over writing is a staple of western intellectual tradition, as Derrida has shown in numerous cases, from Plato to Husserl and Saussure.[5] But with Austin this priority is so crucial – so closely bound up with his authority and influence – that it takes on an almost mythic dimension. Defending the truth of Austin's intentions – perhaps against the letter of his text – becomes in effect a kind of speech-act fidelity resistant to the lures of writing. For indeed, his texts create problems enough when read with an eye to their rhetorical duplicities and blind-spots of logical argument. To read them as Derrida proposes – to refuse, that is, the position of superior Austinian wisdom vouchsafed to his faithful exegetes – is to find them conspicuously failing to perform what speech-act theory would have them mean.

Derrida's essay on Austin was followed up by a 'reply' from John Searle, attempting to correct some of Derrida's flagrant misconstructions of Austin's meaning.[6] Searle points out (among other things) that the 'iterability' of speech-acts is precisely what enables them to hold good – to signify some intelligible meaning – in many varieties of situation. Such was Austin's express intent when he coined his performative parlance, and such is Searle's faithful rendition of the master's authoritative meaning. Searle is not concerned to notice, for instance, how the very word 'performative' carries overtones of a theatrical nature, suggesting that such utterances may indeed be *scripted* rather than issuing from any kind of authentic, self-present intent.[7] This would be to read Austin's text against its own most basic and philosophically-enabling assumption. What is at stake between Derrida and Searle is the issue of speech-act fidelity and, beyond that, the question of *writing* as repressed or occluded in philosophic discourse.

Austin's insistence on the 'serious' (authentic) character of speech-acts is echoed by his commentators when they recollect the single-minded passion and intensity with which he conducted philosophical debates. It is this same attitude which draws the line at performatives uttered on the stage, written down in novels or simply 'spoken in jest'. The common feature of these cases is the fact (as Austin would have it) that they *exploit* the primary conventions of speech-act utterance to create mere replicas devoid of serious meaning. The act of 'performing' the appropriate verbal sequence would then be in danger of moving across, so to speak, from an authentic to a purely theatrical sense. Language would be subject, as Derrida puts it, to a 'generalized citationality', leaving no room for essential distinctions of motive and intent. Such suspicions must at all costs be excluded from speech-act theory; and this imperative extends to the recollected image of Austin himself, as mentor and progenitor.

G. J. Warnock strikes a typical note when he attempts to characterize the peculiar authority of Austin's 'live' performances. Austin, he writes, wanted to treat philosophy as 'more like a science than an art': 'and certainly not one of the *performing* arts; once, when I saw him in the audience of a very distinguished philosophical performer, he found the spectacle so intolerable that he had to go away – and was not himself play-acting in doing so.'[8] One is tempted to ask why the point has to be driven home with such insistence. It is also quite striking that the passage fails to register that curious link between Austin's speech-act terminology and those 'performing arts' which he apparently disdained. To put this down to the workings of semantic repression – at whatever unconscious level – might seem more than a trifle far-fetched. Yet clearly there is a sense in which Austin's writings are 'performances' of the kind which he – and Warnock – would officially banish from philosophic discourse. His texts are by no means innocent of a certain deliberate roguishness or ludic propensity. What is more, they often tend to undermine the very point that Austin has started out (in all apparent 'seriousness') to establish. Such is the case in *How To Do Things With Words*, where Austin sets up what looks like a basic distinction (between 'constative' and 'performative' utterances), then provides a whole series of ambiguous examples which render that distinction untenable. That Austin's texts have this habit of deconstructing their own premises should at least give pause to those who would equate philosophical good faith with the speech-act requirement of sincerely meaning what one says.

But there is another, more fundamental sense in which Austin's writings cannot possibly *enact* the conditions of performative utterance laid down in his explicit statements. The examples which Austin cites are precisely that – isolated speech-acts deliberately taken out of context – and thus fall foul of the basic rule which excludes such artificial instances. The fact that they are *quoted* or *cited* in support of Austin's general argument renders them peculiarly suspect in view of his stated mistrust of such 'etiolated' or 'parasitic' variants. What kind of 'illocutionary force' pertains to speech-acts cited by way of exemplifying speech-act theory? If suspicion attaches to performatives which are merely *performed* – acted, rehearsed or quoted out of context – how can such cases be distinguished from the mass of serviceable instances which Austin calls to witness?

Austin is well aware that writing puts peculiar problems in the way of any 'serious' attempt to formulate the character of speech-act commitment. At one point he remarks quite casually that 'written utterances are not tethered to their origin in the way that spoken ones are.'[9] Few of his commentators see fit to pursue such remarks, or to ask what they imply for a rigorous reading of Austin's texts. The assumption is that his meaning is best grasped – or his intentions most faithfully interpreted – by passing over these local aberrations. This gives rise in turn to the insistence that Austin's writings are in some sense unrepresentative, and his genius enshrined in memories of what he actually *said* on this or that occasion. The ethos of speech goes along with a certain mystique of origins. Thus Warnock again: 'Austin was absolutely first-hand. He was not a purveyor or explainer, however competent or critical or learned, of philosophy; he was a maker of it, an actual origin.'[10] From this point of view Austin's authority is sufficient to check or override any doubts as to the drift of his textual performances. Writing gives way before a sense of privileged access to Austin's intentions, an inside knowledge closely indentified with *speech* as the point of 'actual origin'. What Derrida perceives as the ruling metaphor of western philosophy – the idea of speech as self-present meaning – is nowhere more evident than in the writings of Austin's faithful exegetes.

But this matter of fidelity is precisely what is at issue in Derrida's reading of Austin. His essay could only strike a philosopher like Searle as a monstrous and wilful misinterpretation of Austin's manifest drift. This impression was no doubt confirmed for many readers when Derrida capped the exchange with his massive rejoinder to Searle, exploiting every available device of deconstructionist strategy.[11] What this text sets out to dismantle is the Searlian assumption that a faithful reading of Austin – a genuinely 'serious' reading – can lay some kind of *proprietory* claim to meaning and truth. This would only be the case if speech-act theory were indeed fully valid as Searle understands it; that is, if Austin's authorial intent were unambiguously present in his texts and vested with the power to determine what should *count* as a genuine ('serious') interpretation. But Austin's texts – as we have begun to see – are by no means so single-mindedly serious as Searle would make out. In point of *style* they are often more akin to Derrida's writing than to anything in Searle's (or Warnock's) conception of philosophic truth and authority. In the remainder of this essay I want to look more closely at some of the ways in which Austin's texts subvert – or deconstruct – the 'serious' claims of speech-act theory and philosophy at large.

II

Austin clearly inherits something of the age-old quarrel between philosophy and literature. In Plato, that quarrel had to do with the fact that poets were in the business of feigning, dissembling, propagating mere seductive fictions in the place of philosophic wisdom and truth. It likewise extended to the arts of rhetoric, of sophistical argumentation and of *writing* itself as denounced (in the *Phaedrus*) as a dangerous disseminating medium, a realm of lifeless inauthentic signs.[12] Writing, fiction and rhetorical suasion are identified by Plato as enemies of reason, possessing a seductive power of enchantment which philosophy – in the form of Socratic dialectic – has to overcome. Literature and rhetoric answer that charge in a long succession of texts, from Philip Sidney's 'Defence of Poesie' to Derrida's *Of Grammatology*.

Sidney goes various ways about in the effort to coax Plato down from his position and enlist him where he really belongs, on the side of the poets.[13] Is it not the case that Plato makes regular use of 'poetical' figures and allegories in the furtherance of his own philosophical arguments? And again: might not the poet's 'feigning' – his creation of idealized fictional worlds – be another, perhaps more attractive road to philosophic wisdom? Sidney sets out, in his affable way, to deconstruct the terms of that Platonic tradition which had subjugated poetry to philosophy, rhetoric to reason and (implicitly) writing to speech. His 'Defence' shows a distant but definite kinship with Derrida's essay 'Plato's Pharmacy'.[14] Derrida exploits the techniques of deconstruction to demonstrate the way in which themes of writing and textuality pervade the entire discourse of the *Phaedrus*, disguised but irrepressibly active in the metaphors which structure Plato's agrument.

What exactly is the bearing of all this on Austin and speech-act philosophy? One could begin by taking a lead from that uneasy relation between philosophy and fiction which shows up at various points in *How To Do Things With Words*. It is remarkable how often *novels* figure in Austin's argument, despite his express disclaimer that fictional utterances should count as genuine ('serious') performative acts. One example of 'doing things with words' is the case of signalling the class or generic type to which a particular piece of writing belongs. Such purposes are served 'by the use of titles such as Manifesto, Act, Proclamation, or the sub-heading "A Novel"...'.[15] It might be argued that this is precisely the kind of point that Austin needs to make if performatives in fictional discourse are to be marked off from those which carry real-life entailments and obligations. But it is not so obvious that any such dividing line can be firmly maintained. Take the following remark about the com-plementary act of *closing* the brackets on fictional or other forms of specialized discourse. There is a series of transitions, Austin writes:

> from the word END at the end of a novel to the expression 'message ends' at the end of a signal message, to the expres-sion 'with that I conclude my case' as said by Counsel in a law court. These, we may say, are cases of *marking* the action by the word, where eventually the use of the word comes to be the action of 'ending' (a difficult act to perform, being the cessation of acting, or to make explicit in other ways, of course).[16]

This passage raises all kinds of problems as to the nature, powers and constitutive limits of performative language in general. Clearly its implications are not confined to the peculiar instance – as Austin would elsewhere regard it – of fictional or novelistic discourse.

For one thing, there is the question of how to *distinguish* the point at which cases of conventional marking ('END at the end of a novel') give way to fully–fledged performative acts ('with that I conclude my case'). The passage offers no firm ground or criterion by which to draw such a line. It is far from self-evident that there exists any ultimate distinction between Austin's example of a purely token 'marker' and his instance of a genuine performative. Indeed, his very use of speech-act terminology works to undercut the putative difference. 'Marking the action' is said to pass over – perhaps by imperceptible degrees – into 'the action of "ending"'. This action is somehow meant to possess an authenticating force, or performative intent, absent in cases where a word merely *marks* the act in question. Yet the only real difference between the two examples is the fact that one (putting an END to a novel) has to do with writing and fiction, while the other ('as *said* by Counsel in a law court') concerns an instance of *spoken* language.

Let us put this down to what has already become clear: the affinity between speech-act philosophy and a generalized ethos which equates the primacy of speech with notions of authority, truth and self-presence. Even so, the above-quoted passage from Austin creates real problems of interpretation. The very act of 'ending' is subject to the peculiar difficulty that it has to signal 'the *cessation* of acting', a requirement which makes it, to say the least, an odd sort of marginal case. And Austin's reasoning is equally odd if one pauses to examine its logic and semantics. Those dangerous theatrical overtones seem to be creeping back into performative parlance. An 'act' which marks the end of acting sounds very much like a curtain-call, that peculiar moment of uncertainty as to whether the persons there on stage are still dramatically 'in character' or restored to their workaday professional selves. There is a similar ambivalence about the way Austin's language hovers between an 'authentic' (speech-act) meaning and the kind of artificial 'performance' which that act might serve to mark off or terminate. His text is caught up in a rhetorical exchange of meanings which the logic of its argument seems unable to control. If 'ending' in the full-blown performative sense is 'a difficult act to perform', the problem has much to do with the inbuilt limits and liabilities of speech-act theory. It demonstrates the twist of figural implication which always threatens the performative usage of terms like 'act' and 'perform'.

This same strange logic of rhetorical aberration crops up in various guises throughout Austin's writing. The word END at the end of a novel may be (as Austin suggests) a merely indicative 'marker' devoid of genuine performative force. But where – if that is the case – is the line to be drawn between fictional discourse and the normative conventions which make sense of language *outside* such deviant contexts? The line becomes blurred if 'markers' and 'performatives' turn out to be not so easily distinguishable. As with the curtain-call, there comes a point where fiction and philosophy, stage-acts and speech-acts seem in danger of confusion. The problem is hardly trivial in view of the numerous exemplary fictions and concocted mini-narratives which Austin deploys in the course of his arguments. (A well-known example, from his essay 'A plea for excuses', is the twice-told tale of the shooting of the donkey, designed to bring out the difference between doing something 'accidentally' and doing the same thing 'by mistake'.[17])

J. O. Urmson describes this quintessentially Austinian technique: 'It is important to tell stories and make dialogues as like as possible to those in which we should employ a certain term or idiom in which it would not be possible, or would strike us as inappropriate, to use that term or idiom.'[18] The question remains as to how such a practice might square with the cautionary attitude which Austin adopts toward speech-act instances taken from outside the normal communicative context of utterance. Thus a footnote typically reminds us of 'the possibility of "etiolation" as it occurs when we use speech in acting, fiction and poetry, quotation and recitation'.[19] Yet Austin's exemplary 'stories' would themselves have to be classified as *fictions*, and also – in a generalized sense – as *quoted* (or cited) from ordinary language at large. It becomes less than clear how philosophy can manage to beat the bounds of fictional or literary discourse. And indeed, as we shall now discover, these questions lead Austin into regions of enquiry where literary critics, rather than philosophers, usually take up residence.

In *How To Do Things With Words* Austin makes important use of the distinction between *oratio recta* and *oratio obliqua* (direct' and 'indirect' discourse). These terms are introduced by way of explaining the difference between speech-acts simply quoted – as between inverted commas – and items of reported speech that involve some degree of integral contextualization. Thus: '"You had better not go just now", she said' and 'She advised me against making an immediate departure'. Austin perceives a parallel here with his own distinction between the 'locutionary' and 'illocutionary' aspects of language. The former can be defined – roughly speaking – as the basic semantic or propositional sense of a given utterance. The latter – a refinement of Austin's 'performative' usage – involves the uptake of whatever illocutionary *force* (or speech-act commitment) the utterance might entail. Hence the analogy with *oratio obliqua*; to grasp illocutionary meaning is to penetrate beyond the mere form of words to the operative meaning they convey. Austin's examples are as follows:

> Locution: He said to me, 'You can't do that.'
> Illocution: He protested against my doing it.[20]

The point is to explain the difference, in speech-act terms, between mere quotations (devoid of illocutionary force) and instances of reported discourse where the meaning is grasped and made, as it were, analytically expressive.

Predictably, it is speech in a *fictional* context that Austin singles out as the paradigm case of empty locution. 'This is the "inverted commas" use of "said" as we get it in novels: every utterance can be just reproduced in inverted commas, or in inverted commas with "said he" or, more often, "said she", etc., after it.'[21] In fact there is a further set of distinctions in play by this stage of Austin's argument. Every utterance, he suggests, can be analysed in terms of its 'phonetic', 'phatic' and 'rhetic' components. The 'phonetic' is self-explanatory: 'merely the act of uttering certain noises'. The 'phatic' is perceived as belonging to a *language*, that is to say, a certain recognized semantic and grammatical system. It is only in the 'rhetic' dimension that language achieves, in Austin's terms, 'a more-or-less definite sense and reference'. These distinctions can be seen to complement (or perhaps just to complicate) the existing 'locutionary'/ 'illocutionary' pair. It is only at the level of *rhetic* communication that an utterance can take on any kind of illocutionary force. Whatever belongs purely to the *phatic* dimension is devoid of such determinate meaning and is therefore open – Austin argues – to various kinds of deviant or empty recitation. 'Thus we .nay repeat someone else's remark or mumble over some sentence, or we may read a Latin sentence without knowing the meaning of the words.'[22] Among other liabilities, the phatic act can be mimicked or mechanically reproduced. It can also – as Austin predictably suggests – be placed within inverted commas, like dialogue in a novel.

This shuffling of categorical distinctions is more than a minor quirk in Austin's philosophy. His text seems perpetually at the point of deconstructing its own terminology and working premises. In *How To Do Things With Words* this tendency issues in two major shifts of focus: from the constative/performative couplet to the notions of 'locutionary' and 'illocutionary' force, and thence – as we have seen – to the threefold distinction between 'phonetic', 'phatic' and 'rhetic' acts. And at each stage one is prompted to ask: just *what* is it here in the drift of his argument that Austin is attempting to repress or overcome?

The pervasiveness of *fictions* in his own discourse is perhaps one motive for Austin's continual juggling with speech-act categories. This would include not only those exemplary little 'stories' designed to sort out fine distinctions of usage, but also the sense in which Austin's whole philosophy rests on covert metaphors of narrative technique. One might begin by pointing out that *oratio obliqua* is as common a device in fictional discourse as the forms of *oratio recta* which Austin conveniently rules out of play. The difference, as he sees it, is that direct quotation need involve no evident *grasp* of the quoted utterance, whereas indirect quotation necessarily displays such a grasp. Hence the analogy with mere 'locutions', on the one hand, and authentic 'illocutionary acts' on the other. But this analogy holds certain dangers if pursued beyond the limits established by Austin's fairly casual handling of it. An important characteristic of *oratio obliqua* is the way in which it tends to dissolve any clear-cut distinction between the quoted utterance and the framing discourse which surrounds and comprehends it. Critics of the novel have lately devoted a good deal of close analytical attention to this feature of narrative discourse.[23] *Oratio obliqua* can be seen as a small-scale or localized example of the 'indirect style' which allows the narrator to enter the thoughts of some privileged character and thus create an effective merging or interplay of narrative viewpoints.

This process can be carried yet further to the stage where such distinctions seem to fall away and one finds an imperceptible *merging* of awareness between narrator and protagonist. Such is the 'free indirect style' which plays a large role in Jane Austen's fiction and becomes virtually a staple of modern novelists like Virginia Woolf. Thus, for example:

> Direct: She thought, 'What a perfectly opportune moment.'
> Indirect: She thought what a perfectly opportune moment it was.
> Free indirect: It was such a perfectly opportune moment now.

(The 'now' in this last instance serves to mark it indelibly as narrative discourse, since the word carries a preterite deictic force inconceivable outside such a context.)

These distinctions of narrative style are not just a matter of fashion or technique. They have to do with relationships of *authority* between a framing discourse (that of the implied narrator) and those various thoughts and utterances which issue from other, less privileged sources. At one extreme the narrator assumes an absolute, unquestioned authority in relation to which her characters are 'placed' as more or less knowing or ignorant. (George Eliot might figure as a representative case.) At the opposite extreme is the narrative style which works to dissolve such a firmly hierarchical discourse of interpolated viewpoints. By the same token the reader is refused any secure or privileged position from which to master the novel's meaning. Colin MacCabe makes the point as follows in connection with Joyce:

> A text is made up of many languages, or discourses, and the critic's ability to homogenize these articulations is related to their prior organization within the text.... None of the discourses which circulate in *Finnegans Wake* or *Ulysses* can master or make sense of the others and there is, therefore, no ... dominant position within the text. In Joyce's writing, indeed, all positions are constantly threatened with dissolution into the play of language.[24]

What MacCabe describes here is the radical outcome of a process which begins with the merging of quotation and interpretative context broached in *oratio obliqua*.

It may be, therefore, that Austin's appeal to this division of discourse lands him in something of an awkward position as regards his own criteria for 'serious' or genuine speech-acts. Consistency demands that he maintain a firm sense of the difference between fictional utterances and those produced in accordance with the ground-rules of illocutionary good faith. Yet Austin himself seems increasingly doubtful as to how far such distinctions can possibly hold up. What if the dividing-line between 'literature' and 'philosophy' is merely a species of conventional dictate, vital to Austin's argument but otherwise open to rhetorical deconstruction? What is to prevent the reader from interpreting Austin's text after the manner of MacCabe on Joyce; as reflecting, that is, a discourse devoid of authoritative power where 'all positions are constantly threatened with dissolution into the play of language'? This would in effect make philosophy a branch of applied rhetoric or literary theory, reversing the age-old Platonic prejudice. It would bring out the extent to which speech-act theory depends on the kind of authoritative standpoint assumed by such omniscient narrators as those of George Eliot. What is more, it would raise the question as to whether that 'authority' might be simply one conventional code among others, capable of being deconstructed to lay bare its mode of rhetorical working.

III

This is not in the least a frivolous or mischievous reading of Austin's text. It may nevertheless find special significance in those passages which themselves – often with disarming effect – hint at the non-serious character of Austin's enterprise. Such is the suggestion (predictably seized upon by Derrida) that Austin is out to 'play Old Harry' with traditional dichotomies like 'true'/'false' and 'fact'/'value'.[25] There is likewise the offhand admission that all his philosophizing may be concerned with 'these perhaps not ultimately serious perplexities'.[26] Austin, like Wittgenstein, thinks of philosophy as a therapeutic process which can only claim success if it clears away mishandlings of ordinary usage – specialized *philosophical* mishandlings – and thus, in a sense, puts itself out of business. Yet the kinds of illusion that philosophy creates are oddly interwined with those fictional cases which Austin obsessively explores. They partake, that is to say, of the ambivalent status which constantly insinuates doubt as to the import and 'seriousness' of Austin's arguments. In 'A plea for excuses' he remarks that 'the abnormal will throw light on the normal', this because it helps us to penetrate 'the blinding veil of ease and obviousness that hides the mechanisms of the natural successful act'.[27] But this persistent courting of abnormality tends very often to supplant or infect the 'normal' discourse which it supposedly serves to clarify.

Thus – for instance – one notes in this particular passage the word 'mechanism' as applied to the performance of 'natural' or 'successful' speech-acts. This seems an anomalous usage if one bears in mind the arguments which Austin mounts against merely mechanical or routine forms of illocutionary utterance. The rhetoric of his text again undermines the intended drift of his argument. It begins to look less like a philosophy of 'how to do things with words', and more like a case of how words do unexpected things with what philosophers want to say. Austin points out – again in the context of 'excuses' – that there exist certain words (like 'inadvertent') which lack any corresponding 'positive' term, at least within ordinary commonsense usage. It is a mistake, he argues: 'to assume that the "positive" word must be around to wear the trousers; commonly enough the "negative" (looking) word marks the (positive) abnormality, while the "positive" word, *if* it exists, merely serves to rule out the suggestion of that abnormality.'[28] This passage comes remarkably close to deconstructing the normative basis of all linguistic philosophy. It suggests a strategy akin to Derrida's deliberate dismantling of the structured oppositions (like speech/writing) which dominate the discourse of philosophic reason. In the present context it raises possibilities decidedly eccentric to the general tenor of Austin's arguments. The idea of 'positive abnormality' can be seen as placing a very different gloss on those other 'deviant' instances – writing, fiction, quotation and so forth – which Austin is elsewhere so anxious to exclude.

There are, as we have seen, many instances in his writing of apparently opposite terms which then turn out to exchange characteristics to the point where no such distinction can be firmly maintained. This process of rhetorical substitution runs strangely athwart the logic of Austin's texts. It often gives rise to metaphors suggestive of *disease* or *parasitical* infection. One striking example crops up in a passage where Austin reflects on the awkward liabilities of the constative/performative pair. On the face of it constatives can only be 'true' or 'false', whereas performatives are either 'happy' (= valid, felicitous) or the reverse. Yet Austin is forced to recognize 'that considerations of the happiness and unhappiness type may infect statements (or some statements) and considerations of the type of truth and falsity may infect performatives (or some performatives)'.[29] This rhetoric of 'infection' may remind us of what Derrida has to say about the imagery associated with *writing* down through the history of western thought. Writing as 'parasitic' on speech, as a 'poison' or 'dangerous supplement' – such metaphors have marked the perennial mistrust of inanimate written signs.

Yet it is also a part of Derrida's strategy to show how these metaphors reveal an uncanny double logic which works to reverse their pejorative sense. The 'poison' of Plato's *pharmakon* is also – in terms of etymology and context – the 'cure' or medicine by which philosophy is redeemed. [30] The allegory constructed to denigrate writing can only do so by admitting its indispensability and thus undermining the fable's apparent drift. Likewise with that devious 'logic of the supplement' which Derrida pursues in the texts of Rousseau.[31] Writing is 'supplementary' in the sense that – as Rousseau would explicitly argue – it merely supervenes upon the primary reality of speech. Yet a 'supplement' is also that which *makes up* an existing absence or lack; just as writing comes to figure for Rousseau (or at least for certain of his texts) as somehow more basic and indispensable than speech. In each case a marginal or excluded term is shown to invade the privileged space of its opposite number.

The priority of speech over writing is of course deeply vested in the language and assumptions of Austin's philosophy. It is in line with the principle which elevates speech-act 'presence' as against the problematic detours of fiction or quotation. Yet there is a very real sense in which Austin's philosophical *practice* – as distinct from his local disclaimers – depends absolutely on the evidence of writing. For one thing, his examples of 'ordinary' usage were arrived at by methodically combing through the *Oxford English Dictionary* and compiling whole lists of useful cases – mostly near-synonyms – which might serve to point up some crucial distinction. In itself this procedure has more to do with written than spoken language. A dictionary like the *OED* is based very largely on recorded (often literary) instances which work to codify usage in a manner quite distinct from present-day 'ordinary' speech.

This leads on to the further question of just how closely Austin observes his 'ordinary language' principle. C. 'G. New puts the case as follows:

> Austin recognized of course that ordinary language is not the last word: it can in principle be supplemented and improved on everywhere. But his main contention is that it *is* the first word. We are not entitled to supplement or improve on it until we understand it.[32]

New titles his essay 'A plea for linguistics' and goes on to enter strong reservations about Austin's habit of 'refining' common usage under cover of descriptive analysis. That the word 'supplement' should figure here is more than a passing coincidence. The role of written language *vis-à-vis* speech in Austin's philosophy is indeed a double or *supplementary* role as described by Derrida. Writing, that is to say, is both marginalized as a deviant form of language, parasitical on speech, and held constantly in reserve as the source of Austin's most crucial cases and examples. It figures in his arguments as a kind of textual unconscious, omnipresent in its workings but unable to be recognized as such.

Austin offers various – at times contradictory – answers to the question whether philosophy can 'supplement' ordinary language. In 'A plea for excuses' he argues that 'our common stock of words' embodies the inherited wisdom of ages; that it contains 'all the distinctions men have found worth drawing'; and that these are surely likely to be 'more numerous, more sound . . . and more subtle . . . than any that you and I are likely to think up in our arm-chairs of an afternoon'.[33] This would seem to square with the account often given of 'ordinary-language' philosophy, the version which sees Austin and his followers as aiming at nothing more than the sorting out and clarification of the various senses of words. It is also the target of critics who denounce what appears to them Austin's trifling concern with linguistic minutiae, his disengagement from

substantive philosophical issues and his general (Wittgensteinian) attitude that philosophy should 'leave things as they
are'. [34] His approach has been attacked on political grounds, as
representing a complacent linguistic conservatism, and also by
those in the analytic camp who reject the impressionistic looseness of Austin's criteria. [35]

But there is another side to the 'ordinary-language' picture, as
emerges in that same paragraph from 'A plea for excuses'.
Words, Austin reminds us,

> are not (except in their own little corner) facts or things: we
> need therefore to prise them off the world, to hold them apart
> from and against it, so that we can realize their inadequacies
> and arbitrariness, and can re-look at the world without
> blinkers. [36]

This advertence to the 'arbitrary' nature of the sign is enough to
suggest a complicating tendency in Austin's thought. What
becomes of the appeal to 'ordinary language' if words can
always be 'prised off' the world and shown to be both 'arbitrary'
and (often) 'inadequate'? Language would then indeed require
supplementing to render it fit for philosophical usage. But again:
what can Austin mean when he entertains this notion of seeing
the world 'without blinkers'? Not, surely, that language might
simply fall away, or become ideally transparent, once the
business of refining its subtleties and distinctions had removed
all blocks to understanding. This would involve the naïve idea
that knowledge and perception can attain to a state of pristine
self-evidence entirely independent of language. It would run
directly counter to Austin's most important claim: his belief that
close attention to 'ordinary' language is often more helpful in
resolving knotty problems than any amount of specialized
philosophical argument. Whatever its occasional 'inadequacies',
language is clearly in and of the world, providing as it does our
only means of grasping and interpreting reality.

This ambivalence in Austin's dealing with 'ordinary language'
reproduces what we have seen in his attitude to writing and
fiction. It is a matter, in each case, of his argument requiring
supplementary evidence or support from a source which Austin
can neither dispense with nor fully acknowledge. The repression of fictional speech-acts goes along with the mistrust of

writing; yet Austin's double recourse to 'stories' and the dictionary works to undermine precisely those priorities. The same
applies to Austin's principled but oddly contradictory stand on
'ordinary language'. His appeal to it is meant as a kind of
cleansing operation, a stripping-away of all the mystified verbiage which has grown up around certain (otherwise pers-
picuous) meanings and distinctions. This verbiage accrues from
two main sources. On the one hand it points to occasional
confusions in common usage, confusions which philosophy is
always tempted to 'correct'. On the other, it results from those
very philosophical endeavours – the domain of metaphysics,
epistemology and so forth – which have run up a shaky verbal
edifice of terms to which no real meaning attaches. In this
situation it is hard to know what would count as progress on
either side. Does language set limits and offer practical guide-
lines to the conduct of philosophic argument? Or is it philosophy which gives a hold on subtleties which language – in its
natural state – may be sometimes too crude to comprehend?
Austin's own language seems caught in a perpetual oscillation
between these opposite views.

IV

There is, perhaps, a further associative link between that
primary opposition (speech/writing) and the attitude which
contrasts the wisdom of ordinary usage with the toils of traditional philosophic dispute. Thus Austin argues that one real
advantage of looking at our everyday use of words is that it
draws our minds away from the cluttered pre-history of ideas.
Hence his reason for attending to the topic of 'excuses' and
other such ambiguous or borderline instances of moral debate:

> we can discuss at least clumsiness, or absence of mind, or
> inconsiderateness, even spontaneousness, without remem-
> bering what Kant thought, and so progress by degrees even to
> discussing deliberation without for once remembering
> Aristotle or self-control without Plato.[37]

The canonical writings of past philosophers are seen here as a
burden and distraction from the present business of simply
getting things straight. They stand, one could say, in the same

relation to practical philosophy as *cited* speech-acts (empty forms of words) to speech-acts proper. The subject-matter of philosophy would then be exposed to a kind of progressive 'etiolation', like the various contexts and contrivances which get in the way of illocutionary acts. Thus Austin states his preference for fields of interest that are 'not too much trodden into bogs or tracks by traditional philosophy'. Otherwise it may turn out that 'ordinary language' – or what the philosopher accepts as such – has already become 'infected with the jargon of extinct theories'.[38] In this case prejudice will find an easy foothold under cover of commonsense usage.

It is plain enough to see how this search for new beginnings goes along with the requirements of speech-act authenticity. Philosophic discourse speaks in bad faith if it merely cites or rehearses – with whatever show of novelty – the language and concepts of traditional thought. Philosophy has to enact *in itself* the conditions of authentic illocutionary force which guarantee the tie between words and meaning, sense and intent. Otherwise the philosopher's language is in danger of succumbing to the 'infection' (Austin's metaphor) of a discourse neither his own nor belonging to natural, unperverted usage. Traditional modes of philosophic thought would then fall under the standard Austinian ban which extends to such 'parasitic' cases as poetry, novelistic dialogue and mere quotations-out-of-context.

We have seen to what extent Austin's texts deconstruct their own requirements for speech-act fidelity. They do so mainly by blurring every line between genuine (self-authenticating) cases and the various contexts, pretexts and enabling *fictions* by which Austin builds up his argument. The same sort of question arises with his claim to be releasing philosophy – or at any rate trying to release it – from the thorns and brambles of traditional (philosophic) discourse. This amounts to a secondary displacement of the speech/writing opposition. Ordinary language, on the strength of its (supposed) proximity to speech, is held up as a saving antidote to the deadening influence of *texts* and remote authorities. Philosophic writing falls beneath an alien spell in so far as it enters into commerce with *other* such writings, rather than deriving its best insights from living speech. Austin's vocabulary of speech-act deviance – 'parasitic', 'infected', 'etiolated', etc. – makes up a veritable psychopathology of language and its various ailments. It gains an added resonance from Derrida's numerous examples of the like prejudice in philosophers and linguists from Plato to the present. Living speech is consistently opposed to the dead letter of writing; authentic self-presence to the texts which merely mimic or (worse) disfigure its meaning.

Austin's style does much to reinforce this impression. The speech-feeling comes from its leisurely pace, its self-conscious touches of racy colloquialism and its air of constantly moving off at a narrative or anecdotal tangent. Yet there is, of course, an authorial strategy at work, and one familiar from Plato's dialogues. (Austin himself claims kinship when he recalls, in a footnote, how Socrates 'first betook himself to the way of Words'.)[39] Plato denounced writing but wrote nevertheless, projecting his ambivalent feelings back onto a Socrates whose speech-act integrity could thus be preserved *and* transmitted for others to admire. Austin's disciples can manage something like the same trick. But for Austin's *texts* the situation is more difficult to resolve. The appeal to ordinary language may promise a deliverance for commonsense out of the hands of philosophy and its endless intertextual dialogue. All the same, as more than one critic has noted, Austin's writings – and the very rhetoric of speech-act theory – are themselves shot through with reminders of traditional philosophic issues.

This intertextuality even affects (or *in*fects, to borrow Austin's metaphor) the basic terminology of speech-act analysis. Austin may strive to exorcise the ghosts of Plato and Aristotle from his discussion of everyday ethical parlance. Yet – as Walter Cerf pointed out in a critical review of *How To Do Things With Words*[40] – there is a marked metaphysical flavour about Austin's machinery of speech-act description. It is not, after all, any part of our normal usage to think of certain forms of language as especially fitted to 'perform' certain 'acts'. Behind what appears 'an empirical genus for empirical classification' there lingers – according to Cerf – something more like 'a metaphysical genus for *a priori* ordering'. When Austin speaks of 'acts' or 'performing an act' his terms bear a weight of theoretical assumptions, 'however attenuated this weight is'. Cerf goes on to specify the nature and sources of this lingering influence. The metaphysical weight, he argues, is in part Aristotelian. The concept of act belongs to the group of concepts that are dialectically related to the concept of the potential.... The other part of the metaphysical weight is Cartesian. The concept of act is narrowed down to the *cogito*, over and against material action.[41]

Performative parlance is therefore part of a 'learned and esoteric discourse', that is, if one discounts the vulgar association with 'the language of show and stage'.

Cerf's analysis has large implications for the understanding of speech-act philosophy and its characteristic blind-spots of pre-supposition. What is broached here is a reading of Austin that resists the blandishments of his commonsense colloquial style. It points one way toward deconstructing the belief that philosophy can find, in 'ordinary language', a source of self-authenticating insights and perceptions immune from the beguilements of intertextuality. Writing still exerts a hidden influence on speech, for all Austin's efforts – stylistic and legislative – to exclude such outside interference. With the introduction of speech-act terminology, as Cerf diagnoses it, 'Aristotle and Descartes are ringing their metaphysical bells', even though the sound may by now be so distant that 'our mere wishing not to hear them makes them inaudible'.

This return of the repressed – here in the form of an antecedent philosophic discourse – is yet another sign of Austin's deeply ambivalent strategy. It repeats the same pattern that we have traced in his dealings with fiction, quotation and other such instances of 'etiolated' language. Speech-act integrity is threatened at every point by a textual complicity with themes and figurations which it cannot entirely conceal unless by simply *refusing to write*. Austin's texts can be read as so many allegories and parables of the sheer *impossibility* of doing philosophy on their own express terms. Perhaps the most revealing instance here is the passage which surrenders any claim that certain grammatical forms bear a special or uniquely privileged relationship to speech-act authority. The obvious candidate, as Austin concedes, is the 'first person singular present indicative active'. Here, if anywhere, one might expect to find the home-ground or locus of performative good faith. But Austin has no sooner floated this idea than he snatches it away:

Note that 'present' and 'indicative' are, of course, both
misnomers (not to mention the misleading implications of
'active') – I am only using them in the well-known grammatical way.[42]

Actively and presently *intending* what one says is not to be
confused with the mere grammatical markers 'active' and 'present'. This idea of a link between grammatical form and illocutionary force is just a species of naïve metaphysics. It results,
apparently, from the habit of equating surface structures of
grammar with underlying structures of meaning and intent.

But this dissociating gesture has a more than local and strictly
containable effect. It drives yet another wedge between the
rhetoric of speech-act performance and whatever authentic or
intentional meaning it is assumed to possess. The grammar of
performatives – in this, their most typical first-person guise –
becomes merely a token or superficial index of what they
involve, and in no sense a signal or defining attribute. Hence
Austin's transition, at this point, from examining the logic of
'performatives' to exploring the much vaguer (or more context-
sensitive) field of 'illocutionary force'. It is a gesture we have
come to recognize by now. Grammar is consigned to a merely
accessory role, along with those other props and devices which
Austin makes use of to *exemplify* speech-acts, then discards as
inessential to his purpose. Terms like 'present', 'active' and
'indicative' belong to a conventionalized discourse – that of
grammatical analysis – which cannot correspond with anything
in the nature of speech-act authenticity. Their application in 'the
well-known grammatical way' is itself an instance of language
made over into an alien, 'etiolated' form.

This is the ultimate paradox of Austin's writing. It cannot
begin to formulate its own working language without finding
that language already inscribed in a system of conventions – or
perhaps radical *fictions* – which it then has to exclude on
principle. On the one hand Austin is committed to maintaining
the probity and real-life authority of speech-act utterance. On
the other hand he is everywhere obliged to resort to parables,
analogies and illustrative fictions in order to explain his meaning. The essay on 'Pretending' is evidence enough of Austin's
well-nigh obsessive concern with varieties of inauthentic speech

and behaviour. It patrols the proper usage of the concept 'pretending' in much the same way that 'serious' speech-acts are policed in *How To Do Things With Words*. Take Austin's discussion of the senses in which I may not 'really' be angry, yet still not exactly be 'pretending'. I may, for example, 'be a rough diamond, or have odd manners, or be strangely insensitive, or not be attending to what I am doing: or I may be acting, or rehearsing, or merely imitating, or mimicking'.[43] Thus 'pretending' itself has a genuine dimension to which these instances figure as deviant or non-representative cases. The authentic can only be defined by reference to the inauthentic. And this contrast can always be pushed back a stage to discover different types and species of inauthenticity.

Among the kinds which Austin lists and attempts to distinguish are 'such neighbouring verbs in the family as "affect", "feign", "dissemble" and the like'.[44] Of these, 'feigning' is the word that perhaps comes closest to conveying the peculiar ambivalence of Austin's texts. In renaissance literary usage – especially Sidney's 'Defence of Poesie' – its range of meaning took on the force of a compacted philosophical argument. Poets might 'feign' in the sense of uttering patent untruths, irresponsible fancies dressed up in seductive rhetoric. Such had been Plato's charge against the rhapsodes, an indictment still very much in the air when Sidney came to write his 'Defence'. But poetry also had the power of creating *desirable* fictions, projecting a 'golden' imaginary world in place of an everyday 'brazen' reality. *Feign* and *fain* exchanged senses in a pun which seemed all the more natural for the looseness of contemporary spelling conventions. What the poet feigned (both desired and figured forth) was after all not so very different from that ideal order which philosophers like Plato would *fain* have reality measure up to. Might it not be the case, as Shakespeare wrote, that 'the truest poetry' was 'the most feigning'?[45] The word thus took on a kind of pivotal ambiguity, serving to mediate the rival claims of philosophy and literary criticism.

Perhaps this all seems rather remote from Austin and present-day discussion. Yet Austin's arguments, as we have seen, occupy precisely that ambiguous margin between philosophy and literature, 'ordinary language' and the realm of rhetorical fiction. His interest in *feigning* might appear to be confined to

instances of manifest abnormality, like the cases examined in
'Pretending' and the marginal (deviant) forms of speech-act
utterance. But this normative regime breaks down over and
again as Austin submits it to the process of textual exemplification. Fiction and rhetoric turn out to pervade the very discourse
of speech-act philosophy. Illocutionary utterance may always be
'feigned' if that word is taken in the root sense which links it
both with *fiction* and the idea of *making* something – whether a
promise or a poem – in language. It is in the mazy etymology of
words like these that philosophy and rhetoric have waged – and
continue to wage – their struggle for a privileged relation to
truth.

Of course that desired relation has taken many forms in the
history of philosophic thought. In Chapter 4 I turn away from
the modern linguistic-analytic tradition to consider one whose
quest for authenticity led him through endless ambiguous
detours of fictional inventing. The Kierkegaardian ethos seems
as remote as might be from Austin's quizzical teasings-out of
logic and sense. Yet there is, in Kierkegaard, a similarly
strained, paradoxical relationship between truth and untruth,
good faith and feigning. That such tensions are everywhere
manifest in the texts of philosophy – that they cut across the
deepest distinctions of ethos and period – is perhaps the most
unsettling lesson of deconstruction.

4

Fictions of authority: narrative and viewpoint in Kierkegaard's writing

I

What might it mean to 'deconstruct' Kierkegaard? From one point of view it would produce a reading not only allowed for but actively *pre-empted* by much of what Kierkegaard wrote. His entire pseudonymous production – the 'aesthetic', that is, as opposed to the 'religious' writing – can be seen to deconstruct itself at every turn, remaining always one jump ahead of the *hypocrite lecteur* who thinks to have fathomed its meaning. According to his own retrospective account (in *The Point of View for My Work as an Author*), Kierkegaard was wholly in command of this process from the outset. His 'aesthetic' production was a means of ensnaring the reader in fictions and speculative arguments which would ultimately self-deconstruct, so to speak, at the point of transition to a higher, ethical plane of understanding. The reader would thus be brought to comprehend the inherent limitations and self-imposed deceits of a purely aesthetic attitude to life. This 'ethical' stage would in turn be transcended by a recognition of its own insufficiency in the face of religious experience. Such is the threefold dialectic of enlightenment as Kierkegaard expressly defines it. From the standpoint thus gained atop all the shifting perspectives of Kierkegaard's authorship, the reader will achieve that inwardness of self-understanding which alone constitutes religious faith.

This is how Kierkegaard defends his duplicitous strategies in a key passage from *The Point of View*:

Teleological suspension in relation to the communication of truth (i.e. to suppress something for the time being that the truth may become truer) is a plain duty to the truth and is comprised in the responsibility a man has before God for the reflection bestowed upon him.[1]

The uses of deception are justified strictly by the interests of a higher, self-authenticating truth. 'Reflection' is a highly ambiguous virtue as Kierkegaard describes it. On the one hand it can lead to those fashionable forms of Romantic irony – the endless relativization of meaning and value – which Kierkegaard attacked in the writers of his age. Such was the 'aesthetic' attitude pressed to a dangerous and ethically disabling extreme. On the other hand it provides Kierkegaard with a means of 'teleological suspension', a strategy for conducting the reader through and beyond the perils of ungrounded reflection. He defends himself in advance against the criticisms of those who would condemn such tactics in the name of a straightforward truth-telling imperative. Things being what they are in the present age, the choice must fall between absolute silence and the use of 'indirect communication'. And, given that choice, a timorous silence is scarcely to be regarded as 'a higher form of religiousness'.

The purposes of edification are therefore served indirectly by the detour which leads through various stages of 'aesthetic' reflection. Kierkegaard is at pains to demonstrate that this was all along his guiding purpose, and not just an attitude adopted in the wisdom of hindsight with a view to redeeming his early aberrations. He points to the fact that *both* kinds of production were carried on simultaneously at every stage of his authorship, rather than forming a linear progression which might be equated with the gradual maturing of Kierkegaard's soul. Thus the first ('aesthetic') volume of *Either/Or* was written during the period which also produced the first pair of *Edifying Discourses*. Likewise, toward the end of his authorship, when Kierkegaard's energies were mainly devoted to religious productions, he nevertheless wrote a 'little article' (*The Crisis and A Crisis in the Life of an Actress*) which belonged to the 'aesthetic' dimension. 'The Religious is present from the beginning. Conversely, the aesthetic is present again at the last moment.'[2]

This reversal of normal expectation is repeated in what

Kierkegaard records of his experience in writing *Either/Or*. The first volume (including the famous 'Diary of a seducer') presents an exploration of the aesthetic outlook in all its manifold guises and disguises. The second portion – with Judge William's 'ethical' reflections on the sanctity of marriage – seems to offer itself, in private-confessional terms, as the outcome of the first. Yet in fact, as Kierkegaard reveals, the second volume was the first to be composed, and already bore the marks of his limiting judgment on the 'ethical' as an ultimate philosophy of life. The author at this stage, he assures us, was 'very far from wishing to summon the course of existence to return comfortingly to the situation of marriage'.[3] The implied reference is to Kierkegaard's agonized courtship and final rejection of Regine Olsen, an episode which he saw as confirmation of the need to pass from an ethical to a religious order of existence. So far from implicitly endorsing Judge William's sentiments on marriage, the second volume was written from the viewpoint of an author 'who religiously was already in the cloister – a thought which lies concealed in the pseudonym *Victor Eremita*'.[4]

The ethical stage is thereby deprived of the culminating weight and authority which it might appear to claim if one reads *Either/Or* in terms of a straightforward narrative-confessional logic. Its arguments are already subject to the same kind of qualifying irony, or 'teleological suspension', which works retroactively to frame and disavow the aesthetic attitude. *Either/Or* became a kind of 'poetical catharsis', one which was yet unable to 'go farther than the ethical'. Kierkegaard can therefore return to his work as a *reader* in much the same position as any other, compelled to re-enact its dialectical structure in terms which define his (past and present) relationship to it. This attitude becomes quite explicit in the closing pages of *The Point of View*. 'That I was without authority I have from the first moment asserted clearly ... I regarded myself preferably as a *reader* of the books, not as the *author*.'[5] By adopting this viewpoint Kierkegaard can claim a non-privileged but fully 'existential' encounter with his own previous productions.

It should be obvious by now that Kierkegaard carries decon-struction only to the point where its strategies supposedly come up against an undeconstructible bedrock of authenticated truth. His techniques of 'indirect communication' have a strictly

preludial function, designed as they are to confront the fit reader
with the absolute necessity of passing decisively beyond them.
Self-consciousness and irony exert such a hold on 'the present
age' that truth cannot emerge except by exploiting such ambiguous means. 'Immediate pathos is of no avail – even if in
immediate pathos one were to sacrifice his life. The age has at its
disposal too much reflection and shrewdness not to be able to
reduce his significance to zero.'[6] It is almost as if Kierkegaard
treated the claims of authentic, truth-telling discourse as a
species of mere bad faith in an age so much given over to
'reflection'. He repeatedly fends off moral objections voiced in
the name of what he calls 'a scrupulous and pusillanimous
notion of the duty of telling the truth'.[7] Only by adopting
its own forms of cunning indirection can thought regain
the authentic inwardness lost to an age of aesthetic self-
reflection.

This is of course the point at which Kierkegaard parts company with the present-day avatars of deconstruction. They
would deny what Kierkegaard so strenuously asserts: the existence of a grounding authenticity which can call a halt to the
mazy indirections of language and motive. For a rigorous
deconstructor like Paul de Man, such beliefs are always delusive, a product of the 'normative pathos' which leads us to
assume that language should ideally mean what it says, or say
what it means.[8] Kierkegaard's project depends on his adopting
this sceptical attitude only up to a point, in order to perplex and
finally confound the unbelieving reader. One can certainly find
many passages, in *The Point of View* and elsewhere, which match
de Man by calling into doubt the normative relations of language, truth and subjectivity. Such are Kierkegaard's remarks
on the powerlessness of 'immediate pathos' (or appeals to
self-authenticating belief) in the face of a 'reflective' culture at
large. Deconstruction turns on a similar claim: that thought
should no longer be beguiled into accepting the delusive 'immediacy' of language once the instruments are at its disposal for
dismantling the covert metaphysics at work behind all such
presumptions. For Kierkegaard, however, this work of demystification is always at the service of a higher, ethical or religious
imperative. Deconstruction as practised by conceptual rhetoricians like de Man would surely have figured for Kierkegaard as

a warning example of 'aesthetic' reflection lost in the abysmal regressions of its own creating.

To read Kierkegaard in the knowledge of modern deconstructionist criticism is therefore to face very squarely the choices which his authorship seeks to impose on the reader. The internal dialectics of *Either/Or* are reproduced at every stage of Kierkegaard's writing, the design being always to implicate the reader in questions of interpretative choice which simultaneously force an ethical decision.[9] The unreconstructed aesthete (or purist deconstructor) will read *Either/Or* as a fascinating instance of textual strategies engaged in a shuttling exchange of 'undecidable' priorities. He or she will be impressed by the text's unresolved contradictions of viewpoint, its power to suspend or defer any final, authoritative reading. Its title would in this case be taken to signify the holding-together of two possibilities ('aesthetic' and 'ethical'), without the least need or justification for choosing between them. Yet this response would of course be 'aesthetic' in so far as it refused the absolute choice of priority envisaged by Kierkegaard's authorial design. The alternative *Either/Or* of ethical decision is intended precisely to transcend or discredit any such supposedly facile interpretation. Such a text confronts the 'implied reader' with problems of interpretative grasp more momentous than those usually entertained by current narrative theory. Kierkegaard – to put it crudely – will see you damned if you do not comprehend the innermost, self-redeeming aspect of his authorship.

For Kierkegaard, there is always a decisive moment of advance from 'indirect communication' to truth directly apprehended and thus no longer subject to the ruses and dangers of reflection. To ignore this moment, or wilfully repress it, is to prove oneself lacking in the 'serious' powers of mind prerequisite to higher understanding. Kierkegaard's reader is constantly on trial, required to give evidence of his or her capacity for taking this decisive leap into faith. But Kierkegaard's authorship is equally put to the test, since its very reliance on deceptive techniques might actually mislead and pervert the understanding of a previously well-intentioned reader. Kierkegaard counters this likely objection by making it the *reader's* duty to approach his texts with sufficient 'seriousness' of purpose. Otherwise, he admits, understanding can only

be perplexed and undone by the effects of 'dialectical reduplication' everywhere present in his writing. This is the pivotal point
of encounter between truth and its indirect means of reflective
presentation. The burden now rests with the reader to prove
that Kierkegaard's intentions are not simply lost on his or her
capacities for inward self-knowledge.

Kierkegaard is at pains to justify his position on this crucial
point. His indirect proceedings have to be defended as absolutely necessary if the reader is to grasp the requisite stages of
enlightenment. On the other hand that same dialectical grasp
can only come about on condition that the reader is *already*
endowed with an adequate depth of understanding. As Kierkegaard explains, it is 'the mark of a dialectical reduplication' that
'the ambiguity is maintained'. The unfit reader (one assumes)
may seize on this ambiguity and rest content with its fascinating
play. The elect reader, on the other hand, will respond as
Kierkegaard wishes. 'As soon as the requisite seriousness
grasps it, it is able to release it, but always in such a way that
seriousness itself vouches for the fact of it.'[10] Again, one could
extrapolate something in the nature of an ethical riposte to the
claims of current deconstruction. Harold Bloom has already
pointed to what he sees as the 'serene linguistic nihilism'
manifest among certain of his deconstructing colleagues at
Yale.[11] Bloom's way of coping with this threat – his wholesale
rewriting of poetic tradition in terms of psychic defence and
aggression – is perhaps not an earnest of 'seriousness' in
Kierkegaard's proper sense. But it does partake of the same
desire to *save* the authentic individual – Christian or poet – from
the otherwise endless fabrications of 'unauthorized' language.

Kierkegaard therefore stands in a highly ambiguous relation
to certain current theories of reading and textuality. His authorship presents a double and contradictory challenge to the
claims of deconstruction. It anticipates those claims to a remarkable degree, making Kierkegaard appear at times a kind of
uncanny elective precursor. But it also – and with far greater
'seriousness' – promises the reader a viewpoint which would
render deconstruction at best redundant, and at worst a species
of mischievous 'aesthetic' distraction. The remainder of this
chapter will examine some of the issues raised by this belated
encounter.

II

The deconstructor might ask, to begin with, why it is that Kierkegaard is so often constrained to fall back on distinctly 'aesthetic' parables and metaphors when arguing the case for a higher, non-aesthetic truth. Some striking examples have to do with female sexuality, the image of woman as endlessly seductive, developed in relation to the 'Don Juan' theme in *Either/Or*. Kierkegaard reverts to this metaphor in a passage from *The Point of View* purporting to explain the approach to truth by means of indirection or 'dialectical reduplication'. 'For as a woman's coyness has a reference to the true lover and yields when he appears, but only then, so, too, dialectical reduplication has a reference to true seriousness.'[12] The sexual image retains its hold, not only on Kierkegaard's 'aesthetic' imagination but on the very process of argument by means of which that stage is supposedly transcended. *The Point of View* was written, after all, from the standpoint of one who claimed to reread and comprehend the entire dialectical progress inscribed in his works. 'That I understand the truth which I deliver to others, of that I am eternally certain.'[13] Yet this truth appears still incapable of finding adequate expression without the aid of those 'aesthetic' parables and devices which characterize the earlier, pseudonymous writing.

The 'question of woman' cannot be confined to that single, decisive episode of courtship and rejection in Kierkegaard's private past. That the episode figures in his writing only by indirect allusion – that it belongs, so to speak, to the *vita ante acta* of his authorship – does not prevent it from obtruding metaphorically into the progress of Kierkegaard's arguments. Woman comes to signify, however obliquely, that aspect of dissimulating metaphor and fiction which alone points the way to truth in an age of universal deceit. One is put in mind of Derrida's remarkable pages on the imagery of womanhood in Nietzsche. There emerges a strange articulation of philosophic themes and sexualized metaphor, such that the idea of woman becomes textually intertwined with a deconstruction of 'truth' and its forms of masculine conceptual mastery. Derrida quotes Nietzsche: 'Progress of the idea: it becomes more subtle, insidious, incomprehensible – *it becomes female* . . . .' And he offers the following gloss, drawing on Nietzsche's own metaphorical suggestions:

> all the emblems, all the shafts and allurements that Nietzsche found in woman, her seductive distance, her captivating inaccessibility, the ever-veiled promise of her provocative transcendence . . . these all belong properly to the history of truth by way of the history of an error.[14]

Kierkegaard's uses of 'aesthetic' indirection – especially where the detour passes by way of woman – are likewise subject to a certain ambivalence which questions his assumed dialectical mastery.

One could press the parallel further. Kierkegaard constructs an entire dialectics of disguised confessional intent, designed to vindicate his treatment of Regine Olsen by viewing it from the standpoint of a higher, self-achieved religious wisdom. In *Either/Or* the 'question of woman' is dealt with successively by two powerful ruses of dialectical cunning. The seductress – ever-changing and tantalizing object of 'aesthetic' desire – is mastered by the ethical precepts of Christian marriage, as enounced by Judge William in Volume Two. This provisional ideal is in turn rejected from the 'higher' religious plane of understanding which Kierkegaard claims as his own in *The Point of View* (and which, moreover, he finds implicit in Volume Two of *Either/Or*). Woman is thus thematized in retrospect as the dark side of man's self-knowledge, the source of an illusion which blinds him to the need for transcendence, first to the ethical, then to the religious spheres of value. Kierkegaard's writings enable him to perform an act of self-vindication so complete that it reverses the roles of innocent and guilty, sinned-against and sinning. Whatever the feelings of guilt that may have attached to the memory of Regine Olsen, Kierkegaard's strategy is designed to convert them into causes of his own deepening estrangement from commonplace human affection, and hence his attainment of a true religious inwardness. The confessional motives of Kierkegaard's authorship can thus be represented under the guise of a spiritual progress from stage to stage of premeditated self-enlightenment.

Yet this process cannot entirely conceal the marks of that original repression upon which Kierkegaard's edifying narrative depends. The fact of his self-inflicted break with Regine is everywhere present in *The Point of View*, for all that Kierkegaard strives to consign it to a remote pre-history of misdirected youth. At the figurative level, as we have seen, these reminders take the form of a recourse to sexual-aesthetic metaphors in order to communicate religious truth. Derrida points to a similar emergence of disruptive 'feminized' imagery in Nietzsche's apparently misogynistic writing. Woman, it seems,

> is recognized and affirmed as an affirmative power, a dis-simulatress, an artist, a dionysian. And no longer is it man who affirms her. She affirms herself, in and of herself, in man ... and antifeminism, which condemned woman only so long as she was, so long as she answered to man ... is in its turn overthrown.[15]

Whatever its provision of sustaining alibis, Kierkegaard's narrative still falls victim to the 'dissimulating' power of womanly-aesthetic imagery.

Similar complications surface to vex the idealized projection of his 'authorship' in its self-professed form of a religious education-into-truth. The Regine episode is cryptically alluded to as a 'factum' which Kierkegaard refuses to elaborate, except by stressing its decisive importance and its complex role in the threshold experience which led to his becoming an author. Kierkegaard expressly denies that this experience was *directly* religious. 'I can only beg the reader not to think of revelations or anything of that sort, for with me everything is dialectical.'[16] This disclaimer can be seen as consistent with Kierkegaard's reiterated stress on the element of 'reflection' prerequisite to any vouchsafing of religious truth. But it also serves the more devious *narrative* function of presenting the youthful Kierkegaard as one 'dialectically' removed from the commonplace sphere of human obligation:

> However much I had lived and experienced in another sense, I had, in a human sense, leapt over the stages of childhood and youth; and this lack, I suppose, must be somehow made up for: instead of having been young, I became a poet, which is a second youth.[17]

The 'aesthetic' stage thus becomes the pretext – by a kind of narrative doubling – for Kierkegaard's suspension of ethical judgment as regards his treatment of Regine. As a 'second youth' it effectively stands in for what the narrative cannot directly face without threatening to undermine its own self-approving moral stance. The broken engagement is represented as a crisis, but one which both begins and ends (it would seem) within a kind of 'aesthetic' parenthesis. Only thus can *The Point of View* maintain its precarious narrative coherence *and* the author's claim to moral self-vindication.

Kierkegaard's text therefore works to exclude the possibility of any guilt which might attach to episodes beyond its dialectical control. For all its decisive significance, the event in question is banished to a realm of 'aesthetic' exteriority where it cannot interfere with the author's growth toward spiritual inwardness and knowledge. But the price of this exclusion is a certain persistent ambivalence as to the motives and status of Kierkegaard's self-revelation. *The Point of View* supposedly belongs to the religious and inwardly authenticated portion of Kierkegaard's authorship. It stands alongside such works as the *Edifying Discourses*, where the author speaks (we are to assume) *in propria persona* and without the aid of aesthetic ploys and devices. To read it as a species of fiction would surely represent a perverse disregard of the author's very plain intentions. Yet its handling of the Regine episode – displaced and deployed as it is in the interests of 'dialectical' coherence – suggests the presence of an overriding *narrative* concern. *The Point of View* has this much in common with the typical nineteenth-century novel. The quotidian sequence of mere 'events' is reordered and adjusted to suit the requirements of a well-formed 'plot'. Different viewpoints within the narrative are placed and judged according to the dominant authorial voice. Ideally there should take place a final convergence of interpretative views between 'implied author' and 'implied reader'. The narrative works to ensure this convergence, provided always that the reader proves fit to share its commanding perspective.[18]

Kierkegaard offers precisely such a narrative in *The Point of View*. Yet might it not occur to a different kind of reader – one, say, who questioned Kierkegaard's absolute religious assurance – to detect even here the distinctive signs of fictional representation? Kierkegaard refers to the 'duplex' character of the event

which signalled his religious awakening.[19] In this lay its power
of dialectical development and hence the spur to Kierkegaard's
incipient authorship. But not all 'duplicities' are capable of thus
being channelled into the path of a secure dialectical self-
knowledge. *The Point of View* lies open to a reading which would
question the supposedly decidable choice between 'aesthetic'
and 'religious' modes of understanding. As a self-professed
record of Kierkegaard's motives and intentions, it demands that
one read in good faith and accept its full authenticity. But to
read it as a *narrative* – and one, moreover, which bears distinct
marks of its own very deliberate contriving – is to doubt the very
grounds of Kierkegaard's crucial distinction. By devising such a
perfect sequence of pretexts for his moral life-history, Kierkegaard risks the collapse of his own founding categories. Fact can
no longer be separated from fiction, or 'aesthetic' motivation
from ethical choice. The system of distinctions becomes strictly
undecidable.

Paul de Man has described a similar subversive logic at work
in the text of Rousseau's *Confessions*. The danger of confessional
narratives is that they tend to build up a self-exonerating case
for the accused which leaves him paradoxically with nothing to
confess. Excuses generate a logic of their own which finally
evades the need for 'honest' self-reckoning. 'The only thing one
has to fear from the excuse is that it will indeed exculpate the
confessor, thus making the confession (and the confessional
text) redundant as it originates.'[20] The narrative form permits
any number of face-saving strategies, thus providing Rousseau
(or Kierkegaard) with a means of transforming guilt into a
pretext for displays of redemptive self-approval. At its most
extreme this process can substitute the pleasure of a well-told
tale for the ethical imperative which supposedly prompted the
confession in the first place. Thus, as de Man reads it, 'Rousseau's own text, against its author's interests, prefers being
suspected of lie and slander rather than of innocently lacking
sense.'[21] In Kierkegaard's terms, there must always be a risk
that the 'aesthetic' will return to recapture and distort the
deliverance of authentic truth. De Man describes Rousseau's
textual predicament in words which might just as well be
applied to Kierkegaard. It is always possible, he writes, 'to
face up to any experience (to excuse any guilt), because the

experience always exists simultaneously as fictional discourse and as empirical event'. Furthermore, from the reader's point of view, 'it is never possible to decide which one of the two possibilities is the right one.'[22]

De Man's reading of Rousseau is detailed and compelling, for all its seeming perversity. The central premise is that texts cannot always effectively *perform* what they manifestly set out to *mean*. There is a frequent disjunction between ethical purposes (like the will to confess) and the business of working them out in narrative-textual form. More specifically, there occurs a shift of priorities, such that the reckoning with private guilt becomes subdued to the need for demonstrable public veracity. To confess, as de Man puts it, 'is to overcome guilt and shame in the name of truth: it is an epistemological use of language in which ethical values of good and evil are superseded by values of truth and falsehood . . .'.[23] And these latter 'epistemological' values are compromised in turn by the inherent tendency of confessional narratives to construct a self-accusing penitential stance by way of exhibiting the penitent's remarkable candour. Confessions of guilt become self-exonerating, but also seem to be intensified by the very tactics which serve to excuse them. In short, 'there can never be enough guilt around to match the text-machine's infinite power to excuse.'[24]

Kierkegaard's text is not unaware of this irony lying in wait for its good intentions. At one point the question is explicitly raised as to whether his entire 'literary production' might not be viewed as self-deluded and belonging to the 'aesthetic' sphere.[25] Kierkegaard's defence is curiously unconvincing. Let the reader indeed imagine, by way of experiment, that all his works were composed from the aesthetic point of view. This hypothesis would soon break down when it met with texts (like *The Point of View*) which claimed an edifying purpose. On the other hand, by adopting the contrary hypothesis – that Kierkegaard's entire authorship, including the 'aesthetic' texts, was governed by motives of edification – the reader can see how everything ultimately fits into place. It need scarcely be remarked that this argument rests on a foregone assumption that the reader will accept Kierkegaard's categorical distinctions absolutely at face value. She will accept, that is, the progression from 'aesthetic', via 'ethical' to 'religious' self-knowledege, precisely as described (at the manifest level) in *The Point of View*. Again, it is the fit (or 'serious') reader who thus falls in with Kierkegaard's purposes. But if one reads his text *against* its manifest intentions – alerted to its blind-spots of metaphor and narrative indirection – one may come to entertain a very different understanding.

Had de Man's deconstructionist arguments been applied to Kierkegaard rather than Rousseau, his conclusions would be yet more disturbing. Kierkegaard stakes his entire religious project on the assumption that his writings can effectually convince and convert the reader to a state of inward grace commensurate with his own. Rousseau is at least intermittently aware of the pleasure to be had from shocking the reader by ever more scandalous examples of his 'honest' self-accounting. The air of a 'performance', of frank theatricality, is very much a part of Rousseau's confessional style. For Kierkegaard also, but in a more crucial sense, writing must exert a 'performative' force if it is ever to serve the purpose of communicating truth. It must function both to authenticate the author's meaning – his 'inward' commitment to stand by his words – and to produce a correspondingly inward acceptance on the reader's part. Such performative effects (nowadays the province of 'speech-act' philosophy[26]) are omnipresent in normal language, but they assume a critical dimension of faith to an author like Kierkegaard. His writing cannot entertain any doubt as to its own capacity for winning the reader to an answering state of hard-earned inward commitment.

It is precisely this faith which de Man so upsettingly deconstructs. His reading of Rousseau dissociates 'the cognition from the act', denying that there can possibly exist any genuine, grounding correspondence between linguistic meaning and performative intent. 'If we are right in saying that "*qui s'accuse s'excuse*", then the relation between confession and excuse is rhetorical prior to being intentional.'[27] And again: 'any speech act produces an excess of cognition, but it can never hope to know the process of its own production (the only thing worth knowing).'[28] De Man's argument turns, as we have seen, on the element of *undecidability* which often prevents any clear-cut distinction between ethics and epistemology, issues of 'right and wrong' on the one hand and questions of 'true and false' on the other. And this would be enough radically to suspend the entire existential project of faith upon which Kierkegaard's authority stands or falls.

III

It is Nietzsche who provides de Man with a model and exemplary practice for the strategy of deconstruction. Nietzsche's awareness of the figural dimensions of language, the ways in which rhetoric both asserts and undermines its own performance, form the topic of de Man's most compelling chapters in his book *Allegories of Reading*. Nietzsche deconstructs the claims of philosophy by showing how they rest on an unacknowledged basis of metaphor and figural representation. The most rigorous effort to exclude such devices from the text of philosophy always at some point fails to recognize their buried or covert metaphorical workings. Nietzsche determined to press this insight to the point where it produced an ultimate *aporia* or 'undecidability' with regard to all texts, his own included.

Arguments must always be 'rhetorical' in the sense of aiming to persuade one of their truth, even where that truth attempts to pass itself off as purely abstract and conceptual. Yet rhetoric also has another, self-critical aspect, exploited by Nietzsche in his relentless uncovering of the tropes and devices which philosophers refused to acknowledge in their own discourse. Rhetoric in this sense is the ceaseless undoing of rhetorically persuasive effects. De Man makes the point with elegant concision. 'Considered as persuasion, rhetoric is performative but when considered as a system of tropes, it deconstructs its own performance.'[29] The upshot of a Nietzschean critique of language is to break down the system of decidable oppositions which assign a proper place to ethical judgments on the one hand, and analytic concepts on the other. Nietzsche's 'genealogy of morals' negates every system of ethical values – religious and secular alike – by claiming to derive their precepts from the will-to-power predominant in various phases of language and culture. On a world-historical scale, this repeats the undoing of 'performative' language by the power of demystification vested in the very tropes which compose it. At the same time it admits that any such critique, however 'demystified', must always acknowledge its own *persuasive* (or rhetorical) character. What is so difficult to accept, as de Man writes, is that 'this allegory of errors' (or undecidability) is the 'very model of philosophical rigour'.

Kierkegaard and Nietzsche are often classed together as text-book 'existentialists', thinkers who rejected the great systematic philosophies of their time in order to assert the freedom of individual choice and values. Certainly they shared an aversion toward Hegel, expressed by Kierkegaard in a famous image: that of the philosopher who erects a magnificent edifice of theory, while dwelling himself in a wretched hovel beneath its shadow.[30] Nietzsche likewise saw nothing but grandiose delusion in the claims of Hegelian dialectic. But the two had very different reasons for adopting this negative attitude to Hegel. Nietzsche's objections took rise from a thoroughgoing epistemological scepticism, a belief that Hegel's entire dialectical system was founded on nothing more than a series of metaphors, or figural constructions, disguised as genuine concepts. In Hegel the will-to-power within language achieved its most spectacular and self-deluded form. For Kierkegaard, the case was to be argued on ethical, rather than epistemological grounds. The danger of Hegel's all-embracing dialectic was that it left no room for the 'authentic' individual, the agent of choice and *locus* of existential freedom. Subject and object, experience and history, were all taken up into a massive unfolding of absolute reason which no human act had the power to resist or decisively push forward. Dialectics in this guise was a form of 'aesthetic' aberration, a means of evading responsible choice by setting up a fine philosophical system which the mind could contemplate at leisure.

Nietzsche is decidedly *not* an 'existentialist' in anything like the Kierkegaardian sense. His critique of systematic philosophy goes along with an ethical scepticism more sweeping and corrosive than Kierkegaard could possibly maintain. The Nietzschean 'transvaluation of values' is finally a matter – as de Man makes clear – of deconstructing ethics by way of an epistemological reduction. Nietzsche stands to Kierkegaard as a false ally, one whose undermining of conventional ideas is in the service of a radically nihilistic outlook. Such scepticism is the enemy of true Kierkegaardian inwardness. This antagonism is all the more evident when a critic like de Man draws out the full deconstructive implications of Nietzsche's thought. The effect on his reading of Rousseau's *Confessions* is a measure of their power to subvert every last vestige of 'authentic', truth-telling language. It scarcely makes sense any longer to speak of Nietzsche as an 'existentialist' in the company of Kierkegaard and his latter-day progeny.

Yet to treat this antagonism as a matter of straightforward divergence is to ignore the many complicating factors at work in Kierkegaard's authorship. These take the form – as I have argued – of 'aesthetic' and fictional devices which work to suspend the dialectical progress that Kierkegaard equates with the inward coming-to-truth. The duplicity of language is always in excess of the elaborate strategies which Kierkegaard adopts to explain and justify his authorial conduct. Thus *The Point of View*, by its complex 'dialectical' reordering of memories and motives, creates a text which partakes as much of fiction as of spiritual self-revelation. De Man describes this alienating logic of narrative contrivance as it affects the writing of Rousseau's *Confessions*. 'This threatens the autobiographical subject not as the loss of something that was once present and that it once possessed, but as a radical estrangement between the meaning and the performance of any text.'[31] It is equally impossible to decide just how much in *The Point of View* is dictated by a logic of narrative self-vindication basically at odds with Kierkegaard's idea of existential good faith.

De Man's prime example is the case of 'the purloined ribbon', an episode in which (according to the *Confessions*) a servant girl was blamed for a theft which Rousseau had himself committed.[32] The enduring shame which resulted from his silent acquiescence is supposedly the spur and motive of Rousseau's confession. But the incident becomes – as de Man reads it – a pretext for narrative 'revelations' far in excess of what mere honesty entailed. The plot is further enhanced by the idea that Rousseau (on his own admission) was prompted to betray the girl partly out of motives of obscure sexual attraction and jealousy. But this does not so much acknowledge guilt as generate a further excuse for the excessive display of it. 'What Rousseau *really* wanted', de Man suggests, 'is neither the ribbon nor Marion, but the public scene of exposure he actually gets.'[33] The narrative produces guilt to order and profits in turn from the additional interest thus created.

Kierkegaard is far from wishing to impress by guiltily exhibiting his treatment of Regine. Yet his very reticence on the subject is presented as a form of strategic indirection, a means of bringing the reader to appreciate its crucial significance. Like Rousseau, but more subtly, he *stages* a witholding of vital information the better to guarantee its ultimate effect. What de Man writes of Rousseau could equally apply to Kierkegaard:

> The more there is to expose, the more there is to be ashamed of; the more resistance to exposure, the more satisfying the scene, and, especially, the more satisfying and eloquent the belated revelation, in the later narrative, of the inability to reveal.[34]

The difference between Rousseau and Kierkegaard is one of narrative tactics rather than of demonstrable truth-telling probity. Rousseau 'reveals' his self-incriminating secrets, projecting them back onto a colourfully fictionalized past. Kierkegaard, on the other hand, constructs an exemplary self-justifying narrative which works both to repress and 'dialectically' display its motivating secret.

IV

Kierkegaard thus stands in a highly ambiguous relationship to Nietzsche. The working-out of his standpoint as a religious author necessitates a detour through dangerous regions of thought which bring him close to a Nietzschean position of all-consuming sceptical doubt. This 'maieutic' strategy – as Kierkegaard terms it – holds out a means of awakening his reader from a state of unreflective slumber. But there is always a risk that the method will get out of hand, that the 'aesthetic' production will re-emerge at a stage where its preliminary services are definitely not required. The uses of reflection may not be so easily held within dialectical bounds.

Take the following passage from Kierkegaard's early (pseudonymous) text *Johannes Climacus or, De Omnibus Dubitandum Est*:

> Reality I cannot express in language, for to indicate it, I must use ideality, which is a contradiction, an untruth. But how is immediacy annulled? By mediacy, which annuls immediacy

by presupposing it. What, then, is immediacy? It is reality. What is mediacy? It is the word. How does the word annul actuality? By talking about it.... Consciousness is opposition and contradiction.[35]

The argument has obvious Hegelian overtones, placing subject and object (language and reality) in a constant dialectic of reciprocal negation. It is also much akin to what Derrida or de Man might have to say about the delusions engendered by naïve ontologies of language. Deconstruction sets out to demonstrate that meaning can never coincide with its object in a moment of pure, unimpeded union; that language always intervenes to deflect, defer or differentially complicate the relation between manifest sense and expressive intent. Meaning can be neither straightforwardly referential nor ultimately grounded in the speaker's (or author's) will-to-express. Mediation – or 'reflection' in Kierkegaard's terminology – is the inescapable predicament of language, whatever those pretences to the contrary maintained by poets, philosophers or the normal run of commonsense metaphysicians.

Kierkegaard, of course, entertains this outlook under cover of a pseudonym ('Johannes Climacus'), intended to mark it as a strictly 'aesthetic' and hence inauthentic standpoint. But this tactic again begs the question of an author's power to bracket certain portions or aspects of his work simply by issuing a magisterial fiat in the name of authority and truth. Here, as in *The Point of View*, the issue is undecidable since Kierkegaard's intentions are not unambiguously there to be consulted. What necessity compels us to acknowledge just one of his implied narrators (the 'religious' or authentic), thus consigning the others to a realm of subordinate fiction? As de Man remarks of Rousseau, 'the presence of a fictional narrator is a rhetorical necessity in any discourse that puts the truth or falsehood of its own statement in question.'[36] This applies as much to ethical or philosophic texts as to those which openly or implicitly acknowledge their fictional status. It thus becomes impossible to separate Kierkegaard's authentic authorship from the surrogate identities deployed in its unfolding. Such supposedly clear-out distinctions are the basis for our normal (unexamined) classification of 'literary' as opposed to 'discursive' or 'philosophical' texts. Our readings of the latter are thereby deprived – de Man argues – of 'elementary refinements that are taken for granted in literary interpretation'.[37]

Kierkegaard's writing is peculiarly susceptible to such treatment. It provides all the materials for its own deconstruction in the form of those fictions, 'aesthetic' devices and allegories of reading which make up the larger part of its production. Or perhaps, indeed, that production in its entirety? Kierkegaard undoubtedly labours to interpellate a reader who will find herself obliged to choose once and for all between alternative positions. But his text is unable to *impose* that choice – or even to state its necessity – without in the process seeming to render it impossible. The edifying logic of 'either'/'or' deconstructs into the always available option of removing the disjunctive bar and deciding that decision is beyond reach. In a passage from *The Point of View*, Kierkegaard reflects on the ironies of public misrecognition suffered in the course of his authorship. 'I held out *Either/Or* to the world in my left hand, and in my right the *Two Edifying Discourses*; but all, or as good as all, grasped with their right what I held in my left.'[38] To deconstruct Kierkegaard's text is knowingly and consistently to exploit that everpresent chance of interpretative crossed purposes. At the same time it is only to read Kierkegaard according to a logic of interrogative doubt supplied by the text itself.

Nietzsche's deconstructionist interpreters often cite a passage from his essay-fragment 'On truth and falsehood in an ultramoral sense'. What is truth? Nietzsche asks, and – unlike jesting Pilate – stays to provide an answer to his own question. Truth is:

> a mobile army of metaphors, metonymies, anthropomorphisms, . . . truths are illusions of which one has forgotten that they *are* illusions, . . . coins which have their obverse effaced and now are no longer of account as coins but merely as metal. . . .[39]

The passage nicely exemplifies Nietzsche's epistemological scepticism, his reduction of knowledge and values alike to the status of arbitrary fictions, incidental products of the figurative play within language.

One could set alongside it a strikingly similar reflection from Kierkegaard's *Journals*, written during the final few years of his authorship. Here, if anywhere, Kierkegaard speaks *in propria persona*, with the authentic voice of achieved inwardness. The passage needs quoting at some length:

> What money is in the finite world, concepts are in the world of spirit. It is in them that all transactions take place.
> Now when things go on from generation to generation in such a way that everyone takes over the concepts ... then it happens only too easily that the concepts are gradually changed,.... they become like false coinage – while all the time all transactions happily continue to be carried out in them.... Yet no one has any desire to undertake the business of revising the concepts.[40]

Up to a point the metaphors work to similar effect. Nietzsche and Kierkegaard each perceive a process of conceptual devaluation at work within the handing-down of knowledge and truth. They both attribute this process to the way in which meanings are mindlessly accredited as tokens of a currency subject to no kind of validating issue or control. But where Kierkegaard treats this as a symptom of latter-day cultural malaise – a measure of spiritual inanition – Nietzsche regards it as inevitable, given that all truths and values are arbitrary constructs from the outset. Kierkegaard is still able to imagine a decisive 'revision' of values, taken on by the few elect individuals whom Providence singles out for the task. No such intervention is possible for Nietzsche, since the concepts of truth and falsehood are so closely inter-twined that thought must be deluded if it hopes to re-establish them on a proper, authentic basis.

This is to state Kierkegaard's difference with Nietzsche as it would strike a convert or implicitly *believing* reader. But again, his argument seems obliged to pass through a detour of strategic indirection which leaves itself open to further deconstructive reading. Under present conditions the Christian 'reviser' cannot assume the self-evident truth vouchsafed to an 'apostle'. His way must necessarily partake of duplicity and fiction:

> If the apostle's personal character is one of noble and pure simplicity (which is the condition for being the instrument of the Holy Spirit), that of the reviser is his ambiguous know-ledge. If the apostle is in a unique and good sense entirely in

the power of Providence, the reviser is in the same power in an ambiguous sense.[41]

Again the question presents itself: how can limits be set to the dissimulating power of this 'ambiguous' knowledge? What is to vouch for these tactics being ultimately on the side of inwardness and truth? The passage provides an answer in the form of that Providence which everywhere governs Kierkegaard's design and underwrites his authorial good faith even where it suffers the necessary swerve into conscious double-dealing. Yet Providence itself appears unable to distinguish such religiously motivated tactics from the general run of deceit and delusion. In the place of true 'apostles' there nowadays come only 'connoisseurs in dishonesty', and they – since they are a part of the 'general dishonesty' – are treated alike by Providence as 'ambiguous creatures'.[42]

Kierkegaard's text thus goes to quite extraordinary lengths to make trial of its own most crucial assumption. By the end of his journal entry the argument has come round to the point of implicitly endorsing *Nietzsche's*, rather than Kierkegaard's own deployment of the monetary image. Or – what amounts to the same thing – it has effectively denied the possibility of deciding between them. Any restoration of authentic truth achieved by the Christian 'reviser' can only appear under the worldly guise of dissimulating 'ambiguity'. If genuine inwardness exists, its credentials are self-evident only to the true believer, and are not to be vouchsafed by way of communicable argument. Nietzsche's contention – that the coinage of truth is always already a devalued and fraudulent currency – seems to infect the very logic of Kierkegaard's argument.

Deconstruction is indeed the devil's work when applied to an author like Kierkegaard. It seeks to undermine conventions of interpretative tact which authority would have us believe are more than just 'conventions', providing as they do the very basis of authoritative utterance. Kierkegaard's commentators may disagree as to the best or most fruitful way of interpreting his work. Where some declare in favour of a largely biographical approach, others argue that the writings are more complex and elusive than any meaning conferred on them by the life. There are likewise differences of opinion as regards the relative importance of Kierkegaard's pseudonymous works, or their place and dialectical function within his authorship as a whole.[43] Nevertheless, there is a powerful normative assumption which unites these otherwise divergent views. The commentators' proper concern is always to *expound* an author's texts in obedience to the deep-lying purposive intent which serves to justify both his work and theirs. Kierkegaard's appeal to 'providence' – his faith in an end to the duplicities of language – is thereby reproduced in his interpreters. Deconstruction breaks with this providential ethics of reading. It affirms the irreducibility of writing to any preconceived idea of authorial design. In Kierkegaard it meets perhaps the highest and most resourceful challenge to its powers of textual demystification.

5

Image and parable: readings of Walter Benjamin

I

Marxist literary criticism is a house with many mansions; most of them claiming a privileged access to the great central chamber of history and meaning. Only the most blinkered polemicist could nowadays attack 'Marxist criticism' as if it presented a uniform front or a clearly delineated target. Differences of outlook have developed to a point where debates within Marxism are often more highly charged and polarized than anything brought to bear by its downright opponents. These differences will seem a crippling liability only from the viewpoint of a hard-line determinist creed which insists on the rightness of its own reductive methodology, coupled to a single-track notion of historical necessity and change. The alternative, as New Left theorists have argued, is to examine the diversity of present-day Marxist thinking and show how its various traditions take rise from various backgrounds of political and cultural development. Perry Anderson's *Considerations on Western Marxism* (1976) is one such attempt to 'situate' the work of thinkers like Sartre, Althusser and Adorno in terms of their beleaguered position as Marxist intellectuals outside the active mainstream of any revolutionary movement.

Another is Terry Eagleton's *Criticism and Ideology*,[1] a book which set out to rethink the bases of a Marxist-theoretical approach to English literary history. Eagleton, like Anderson, takes it as axiomatic that no such critique can get under way without first coming to terms with the problems and dilemmas which others have faced in trying to make new sense of a communal enterprise. For Eagleton this means a diagnostic treatment of the gaps and significant silences which have marked the texts of those – like Arnold or Leavis – engaged in a class-based mystification of literary history and values. The critique extends to what Eagleton sees as the inbuilt problems of a homespun British Marxism, whether of the crudely determinist variety (Caudwell) or the 'left-Leavisite' amalgam of radical themes and traditionalist assumptions represented by Raymond Williams. Eagleton's approach lays claim to a power of unmasking the latent ideology at work both in literary and critical texts. Rather than simply collapse that distinction – as desired by the current post-structuralists, with whom he is wholly out of sympathy – Eagleton strives to articulate the different structures and relations of discourse which situate criticism *vis-à-vis* literary history. He proposes a Marxist 'science of the text' which would bring out its ideological modes of production, inscribed in the twists and unconscious blind-spots of meaning where a project comes up against its own impossibility. Criticism 'deconstructs' the literary text, but not (like certain of the Yale deconstructors) with a view to breaking down all possible distinctions between literature and commentary, merging both in the open-ended freeplay of signs. For Eagleton there is indeed a knowledge of the text which stands at a definite remove from its object, just as literature itself 'works' and transforms the raw stuff of lived ideology, thus offering it up to critical knowledge.

Eagleton's theory of literary production was worked out in response to a powerful new current of Marxist thought, associated mainly with the French philosopher Louis Althusser. What this programme involved, very briefly, was a rigorous re-reading of Marx's texts, aimed at defining their precise theoretical structure and the place within them of such concepts as 'knowledge', 'ideology' and 'structure' itself. Only thus could Marxist science attain the clarity and grasp of its own first principles which would set it apart from other, deviant or 'ideological' discourses. This meant drawing a firm critical line (or 'epistemological break') between the early, humanist Marx and the later productions – including *Das Kapital* – where his thought took on the full rigour of its scientific basis. Such a theory, in Althusser's words, 'makes it possible to distinguish a word from a concept, to distinguish the existence or non-existence of a concept behind a word, to discern the existence of a concept by a word's function in the theoretical discourse ...'.[2] This structuralist reading of the Marxist text is intended as an immanent critique, a means of salvaging the essential Marx from those elements in his thought which remain partly captive to ideological motifs.

Eagleton follows Althusser in his elaborate account of the various levels and productive transformations involved in the passage from lived ideology to critical knowledge. The literary 'mode of production' is seen as occupying a kind of midway position between the 'vivid but loose contingencies' of everyday belief and the standpoint of a Marxist science which can break with all such ideological representations. Literary texts are the source of a knowledge which they themselves can never self-consciously attain to, but which they alone make possible by virtue of their mediating forms and revealing contradictions. Just as literature is no mere reflex image but a potent reworking of ideological themes, so ideology itself – on Althusser's terms – plays ah active role in the shaping of political awareness. Ideology 'precedes the science that is produced by making an epistemological break with it, but survives alongside science as an essential element of every social formation, including a socialist and even a communist society'.[3] Hence the *ensemble* of relations – ideology, literature, critical science – which Eagleton raises to such a high point of conceptual definition.

Althusserian Marxism has come increasingly under attack during the past few years. The historian E. P. Thompson has denounced what he sees as the monstrous abstract machinery of a self-styled 'science' totally divorced from the human realities of history and politics. In his essay 'The poverty of theory' Thompson combines a broadside polemic with a shrewd undermining of the whole conceptual edifice of Althusserian philosophy.[4] What this really amounts to, he argues, is a desperate retreat from lived experience into a form of scholastic argumentation where supposedly 'materialist' concepts and themes are run up into a shaky but doctrinaire structure of assumptions. Thompson writes from an expressly Marxist-humanist standpoint, as one of those whom Althusser's 'science' would consign to the useful but pre-critical labours of 'ideological' practice. His essay has been largely ignored by the

Althusserians, or treated with mild disdain as a spirited riposte from the adversary camp. More decisive perhaps are the internal tensions and signs of revolt which have come to the surface in recent 'post-Althusserian' discussion. Thompson's polemics find an echo in the widespread feeling, on the current New Left, that theory – or a certain brand of intransigent and self-sustaining theory – has pushed its claims too far and stands in need of thorough reassessment. These misgivings have to do mainly with Althusser's rigid distinction between science and ideology, his habit of assuming that thought can arrive – by a kind of structural auto-critique – at the hidden constraints of ideological misrecognition. To reject this rationalist (some would say idealist) structure of ideas is to envisage a very different role for Marxist criticism and theory of culture.

II

Eagleton's writings since *Criticism and Ideology* have reflected this growing disenchantment with the promise of Althusserian theory. A more recent book is devoted to the German-Jewish critic and philosopher Walter Benjamin,[5] a figure whose standing among Marxist critics has grown inversely with the waning of Althusser's influence. The reason is not far to seek, since Benjamin represents an alternative vision, a Marxism rife with contradictions and paradox but freed from the narrowing rationalist dogma which Althusser is felt to impose. Benjamin's elusive temperament entered into everything he wrote, even at the time when Brecht's hard-headed influence was running strongly counter to his own mystical-contemplative leaning. That temperament is at once a source of appeal and a constant temptation (as the Marxist sees it) to those who would appropriate Benjamin's work in the service of a mystified cult ignoring its materialist motives. Hence the often bitter controversies which have surrounded the editing and belated reception of much of Benjamin's output. Eagleton makes this position very clear in his polemical introduction. To write about Benjamin is not to engage in theoretical refinements on a body of texts whose political safe-keeping is entrusted to a like-minded few. Such was perhaps the case with Althusser, but not when it comes to the complex, many-levelled writings of a thinker like Benjamin.

Rather it is a question of wrenching them away from passive absorption into a mainstream culture which can all too easily seize on their conformable aspects.

Benjamin himself provides the images and strategies for the kind of revolutionary criticism which – as Eagleton argues – can alone rescue his thought from useless mystification. He presents the interpreter with problems which cannot be resolved by the mere application of ready-made 'dialectical' categories. Benjamin's historical pessimism – everywhere present in his reflections on culture and tradition – holds out against the kind of 'enlightened' Marxist thinking which draws a too facile equation between knowledge and progress. To Benjamin, history is far from unfolding in the great intelligible sweep of continuity which Hegel – and a certain Marxist tradition – would seek to comprehend. His sense of the relation between past and present is shot through with Benjamin's typical ambivalence, his mixture of messianic craving and a melancholy knowledge of the oppression, the weight of injustice and suffering, borne down by history. Tradition for Benjamin can only be redeemed through moments of wholly unprecedented insight where the past takes on a transfigured significance *despite* and *against* the historical stream of events. Every monument of culture, he wrote, is simultaneously and by its very nature a monument to barbarism. Tradition is in the keeping of the powerful, the oppressors, just as history is written by the conquerors and never by the conquered.

This is the burden of Benjamin's famous 'Theses on the philosophy of history', a sequence of eighteen aphoristic statements which seem calculated to tease commentary almost out of thought. Benjamin's theses are couched in style which draws in equal measure on the language of dialectical materialism and the images of time and revelation hallowed by Jewish mystical tradition. On the face of it their message is a bleak historical pessimism which only makes contact with Marxist thought in a negative way, by bringing home the waste and human desolation which litters the wake of history. Yet it is possible to read them as redemptive parables, not by ignoring their pessimistic vision but by glimpsing its other face, a utopian impulse which survives all the ravages of time. This twist of implication is finely captured in his passage on the 'Angelus Novus', a painting by

Paul Klee which Benjamin owned and often returned to as a kind of talismanic image:

> This is how one pictures the angel of history. His face is turned toward the past. Where we perceive a chain of events, he sees one single catastrophe which keeps piling wreckage upon wreckage and hurls it in front of his feet. The angel would like to stay, awaken the dead, and make whole what has been smashed. But a storm is blowing from Paradise; it has got caught in his wings with such violence that the angel can no longer close them. This storm irresistibly propels him into the future to which his back is turned, while the pile of debris before him grows skyward. This storm is what we call progress.[6]

This brooding transformation from image to parable conveys the complexities of Benjamin's thought with a force unattainable in precept or theory. To read it as a gesture of despair, a gloomy acquiescence in the universal nightmare of history, is clearly to ignore its manifold implications. What the image suggests most strongly is the way in which utopian longings can be kept alive precisely by renouncing the 'enlightened' belief in history as a universal progress from darkness to light. Such totalizing concepts are for Benjamin the property of those who have commandeered culture and tradition, stamping their image on all that remains of a 'monumental' past. To break the stifling hold of that tradition is to bring a melancholy gaze to bear on the 'wreckage' which surrounds the triumphant procession of culture.

Benjamin's fascination with ruins – physical and allegorical – went along with his catastrophist philosophy of history, his sense that meaning had to be violently wrested from the bland continuity of tradition. This connects in turn with one of Benjamin's favourite literary themes, that of the *flâneur* or compulsive street-walker, parrying the shocks of modern urban existence and making himself at home in the anonymous crowds. Baudelaire was the model of this curious vocation, and one of Benjamin's most cherished projects was his study of Baudelaire, 'the lyric poet in the era of high capitalism', seen against the backdrop of the Second Empire and the Parisian arcades.[7] This side of Benjamin's temperament, the dreamy-melancholic, existed in a constant productive tension with the drive to understand and demystify the alienated forms of modern awareness. From Brecht he took the lesson that theory often needed to be fortified with a certain tough-mindedness in practical matters, where too much refinement could only distract from the task in hand. This *plumpes Denken* (perhaps best translated as 'rough-and-ready thinking') comes across in Benjamin's reported dialogues with Brecht and his writing on the uses of drama and poetry as instruments of political change. But there is always a sense of ironic reserve on Benjamin's side, his admiration for the artist as man-of-action tinged with a rueful knowledge of his own more reclusive and complex temperament.

This tug of commitments is nowhere more evident than in Benjamin's classic essay 'The work of art in the age of mechanical reproduction'.[8] His theme is the impact of mass-produced or replicable art-forms on the nature of aesthetic experience in general. Benjamin sees the advent of photography and film (to take the most obvious examples) as marking a decisive shift in the relations of cultural production and reception. Where art is inescapably caught up in the process of commodity exchange it loses its traditional 'aura', the quality of self-possessed uniqueness which had hitherto set its stamp on the 'authentic' masterpiece. Benjamin is far from waxing nostalgic over this invasion of culture by the instruments of modern technology. He shows small patience with those who would redeem the situation by investing film with the qualities of 'art', giving it a ritual dimension absurdly out of keeping with its mechanical nature. The reproducibility of artworks is for Benjamin an index of the extent to which politics – the struggle for possession of cultural goods – has displaced the purely 'aesthetic' realm of contemplation. Attempts to revive that mystique are denounced as a reflex of outworn cultural piety, a gesture of thinly veiled political reaction. To 'aestheticize politics' is to fall into an attitude of elitist nostalgia which Benjamin refuses to countenance. The only alternative, he argues, is a willed acceptance of the opposite phenomenon, the need to 'politicize aesthetics'.

Benjamin's loyalties at this stage are thus firmly pinned to the materialist belief in socio-economic conditions as the ultimate determinants of meaning and value. In essays like 'The author as producer' he stresses the need for revolutionary art to seize and exploit the available means of production, toppling the artist from his privileged 'creative' position and involving him perforce in the workaday mechanics of his craft. The crucial point, Benjamin argues,

> is that a writer's production must have the character of a model: it must be able to instruct other writers in their production and, secondly, it must be able to place an improved apparatus at their disposal. This apparatus will be the better, the more consumers it brings into contact with the production process – in short, the more readers or spectators it turns into collaborators.[9]

The prime example here is of course that of Brechtian theatre, with its deliberate design to 'alienate' the audience, forcing them to think about what is happening on stage by refusing them the comforts of an easy emotional identification. Benjamin extends this ethic of constructive detachment to the entire modern sphere of cultural relations. He rejects the ideology of genius which sets up the artist as an inspired creator of unique, unrepeatable works. In its place Benjamin calls for an effort of practical engagement and transformation, involving not only the work itself but all those cultural institutions – theatre, film, printing technology – which determine the extent of its public availability.

There is no doubting Benjamin's commitment to this materialist aesthetic. To some of his commentators – notably Gershom Scholem – Brecht's was in the main a harmful influence, a heavy-handed dealing with Benjamin's ideas which forced them into the narrow track of Marxist dialectics. Scholem speaks for the tradition of Jewish-mystical scholarship and exegesis which has struggled – understandably – to rescue Benjamin's thought from the clutches of Marxist theory. George Steiner seems to share this perspective in a passage which Eagleton quotes disdainfully as a typical instance of kidnapping tactics from the right. According to Steiner:

> Benjamin would doubtless have been sceptical of any 'New Left'. Like any man committed to abstruse thought and scholarship, he knew that not only the humanities, but

humane and critical intelligence itself, resides in the always
threatened keeping of the very few.[10]

Steiner's elitist characterization goes against the grain of much
in Benjamin's explicit writing on politics, culture and the role of
the modern intellectual. Yet it does undeniably answer to a deep
ambivalence in Benjamin's thought which Eagleton himself – in
less polemical moments – is quick to acknowledge and explore.
Benjamin's commitment to Marxist-materialist themes is never
far distant from his brooding awareness of the sacrifice involved
in yielding up tradition to the pressing demands of the moment.
The loss of cultural 'aura' which Benjamin describes may be a
necessary process and a portent of hope if correctly diagnosed.
Yet it still carries a charge of nostalgic reverie, disguised only
partially by Benjamin's crisply phrased Brechtian maxims.

This conflict of motives seems close to what William Empson
described in the opening chapter of *Some Versions of Pastoral*
(1935). Empson compared the pronouncements of Socialist
Optimism with the feeling implicit in much tragic literature, that
no political system can overcome the 'waste and isolation' of
individual suffering. Empson's extended definition of pastoral
was based on the ironies produced by this encounter between
the 'complex' individual and the 'simple' requirements of objective social justice. The tone is set by the opening discussion of
Gray's 'Elegy', which Empson reads as a rich but confused
example of 'bourgeois ideology' up against the facts of class
inequality. The poem muses on themes of misery and failed
aspiration, treating them with a 'massive calm' which implies
that no amount of political engineering could do much about
them. While seeming to understand 'the considerations
opposed to aristocracy', it finally comes out against them by
adopting a tone of stoic impersonal clam, suggesting 'that we
ought to accept the injustice of society as we do the inevitability
of death'. Empson admits that there is something repellent – a
'cheat in the implied politics' – which has caused many readers
to dislike the poem, without quite knowing why. And yet,
Empson thinks, there is a truth in Gray's sentiments which
cannot be put down to mere ideological self-interest:

> It is only in degree that any improvement of society could
> prevent wastage of human powers; the waste even in a

fortunate life, the isolation even of a life rich in intimacy, cannot but be felt deeply ...[11]

Pastoral, as Empson conceives it, expresses this sense of inescapable unfulfilment, the fact that no social order can really match up to the complex aspirations of the 'gifted' individual.

Marxists have often – and with reason – found something deeply suspect in the pastoral convention. Empson is aware of this resistance, and indeed meets it more than halfway in his remarks on Gray's 'cheating' rhetoric. But he also sees problems with the current dictates of Soviet 'proletarian' art (*Some Versions* was published in 1935), quoting from a speech by Maxim Gorky as evidence of the tensions still unresolved in Marxist philosophy of art. Gorky offers a simplified formula for socialist realism, requiring that the actual be 'supplemented' by the desirable, things as they are transformed by revolutionary zeal. Empson's reaction needs quoting at length:

> When communists say that an author under modern capitalism feels cut off from most of the life of the country, and would not under communism, the remark has a great deal of truth, though he might only exchange a sense of isolation for a sense of the waste of his powers; it is certainly not so completely true as to make the verse from Gray pointless to a man living under communism.[12]

This effort to see both sides of the question – to hold them in an attitude of open-minded tolerant understanding – is itself bound up with the pastoral complex of feelings which Empson is trying to describe. To a Marxist it would look like plain political cheating, a latter-day version of Gray's covert propaganda.

All the same it is striking how close are the parallels between Empson's 'pastoral' and the predicament of the modern artist-intellectual as suggested by Benjamin's writings. The 'Conversations with Brecht' are a case in point, with Benjamin adopting a tone of pensive non-resistance which often leans over into good-humoured irony. Various of Benjamin's projects – like the essay on Kafka – are criticized by Brecht for their arcane or 'mystifying' tendency, then quickly dropped as a topic of conversation, only to resurface later when Benjamin's defences have been privately pulled together. Brecht brings everything down to the level of homely parable, chiding Benjamin's habit of 'deep' interpretation. ('Depth doesn't get you anywhere at all. Depth is a separate dimension, it's just depth – and there's nothing whatsoever to be seen in it.')[13] Benjamin broods on these criticisms, noting to himself that 'penetrating into depth is my way of travelling to the antipodes'. Brecht is always given the last word, though sometimes his commonsense practicality bears more than a hint of the banal.

'Putting the complex into the simple' is how Empson describes the root strategy of pastoral. The same phrase could be applied to the lessons in tactical thinking and 'crude' dialectics which Benjamin took from Brecht. But along with those lessons Benjamin absorbed a habit of reserve and laconic self-containment which comes across clearly in his dealings with Brecht. This is the other half of the pastoral equation, the spirit of self-protective irony which enables the 'complex' individual to square his imaginative needs with the pressures of society at large. In Benjamin's case it was a temperament nurtured on the high traditions of German art and speculative philosophy, thrown into conflict with a Marxist creed which – at least in its Brechtian activist form – had little time for such things. Benjamin suffers with peculiar intensity the conflict which Empson traced, from its relatively simple and unselfconscious beginnings (the renaissance courtier-as-swain) to its modern guise in the alienated artist-as-victim. One further passage from Empson may help to bring the analogy home. Pastoral, he writes, is often based on the assumption that

> some people are more delicate and complex than others, and that if such people can keep this distinction from doing harm it is a good thing, though a small thing by comparison with our common humanity.[14]

It is for reasons like this, he continues, that 'the most valuable works of art so often have a political implication which can be pounced on and called bourgeois.'

III

A Marxist commentator might be inclined similarly to pounce on the 'bourgeois' elements in Benjamin's thought with a view to winnowing out its usable materialist content. This attempt could proceed along two different lines. It would either be a question of marking off the early 'idealist' Benjamin from his later Marxist development, or of taking his work as a whole and subjecting it to a thoroughgoing materialist critique. The first of these alternatives runs up against a problem in the fact that Benjamin's thinking never entirely broke with its Jewish-speculative background, even (as we have seen) at the time when Brecht's canny influence was exerted to maximum effect. Metaphysical themes are so closely intertwined with materialist motives that it becomes impossible to draw them apart as stages in Benjamin's development. Most of his commentators (Eagleton among them) have taken the second line, and offered a shrewdly materialist gleaning of Benjamin's various texts. To his sympathetic readers on the current New Left, Benjamin presents both a challenge and a sense of welcome creative enlargement after the abstract rigours of Althusserian theory. For Fredric Jameson (in *Marxism and Form*) he figures expressly as a mediating angel between materialist criticism and the Jewish tradition of visionary-utopian thought.

Jameson argues for an integrated reading which would draw out the full revolutionary charge of Benjamin's melancholy texts. He quotes from a remarkable letter in which Benjamin describes his contemplative and deeply allegorical turn of mind:

> I have never been able to enquire and think otherwise than, if I may so put it, in a theological sense – namely in conformity with the Talmudic prescription regarding the forty-nine levels of meaning in every passage of the Torah.[15]

Jameson glimpses the prospect of a fruitful liaison between Marxist criticism and the practice of allegorical reading envisaged by Benjamin. He goes so far as to claim that the traditional four dimensions of scriptural exegesis (literal, moral, allegorical, anagogical) can each be transposed to a Marxist perspective 'replacing theology with politics'.

Jameson's theme is the tension in Marxist aesthetics between a 'negative hermeneutic' which deconstructs the forms of ideological mystification, and a positive or 'utopian' impulse which keeps alive the image of human fulfilment. In Benjamin he sees this tension projected onto the complex, paradoxical relationship between 'aura' and 'allegory'. Where the one exerts a nostalgic hold upon Benjamin's brooding temperament, the other intervenes as a constant reminder of the fragmentary, discrete perceptions offered up to modern understanding. Allegory is the mind's response to a world of objects deprived of inherent significance and value, such that their meaning flashes up only in moments of intermittent grasp. Jameson describes this condition most succinctly:

> Aura is in a sense the opposite of allegorical perception, in that in it a mysterious wholeness of objects becomes visible. And where the broken fragments of allegory represented a thing-world of destructive forces in which human autonomy was drowned, the objects of aura stand perhaps as the setting of a kind of utopia ... not shorn of the past but having absorbed it, a kind of plenitude of existence in the world of things, if only for the briefest instant.[16]

It was the image of this fleeting utopia, this instant wrenched from the numbing procession of history, that Benjamin discovered and cherished in the painting by Klee.

Eagleton likewise stresses the close affiliation in Benjamin's thought between allegory and the 'fallen' or alienated character of secular language and representation. He devotes an illuminating chapter to Benjamin's early work on the German *Trauerspiel*, a seventeenth-century dramatic form much akin to the English revenge tradition.[17] This was Benjamin's *Habilitationsschrift*, a thesis intended to secure him a place in the German academic system. That it failed to do so – rejected out of hand by the baffled Professor of Aesthetics at Frankfurt – is hardly surprising given the extreme complexity and introverted structure of Benjamin's text. He discovers in the *Trauerspiel* a reflected image of the melancholy homeless condition which afflicts the present-day interpreter. Benjamin was writing partly under the influence of German Expressionism, which he saw as in some sense a modern counterpart of the alien, buried tradition unearthed by his scholarly researches. More specifically, he treats the *Trauerspiel* as a veritable storehouse of emblematic signs and tokens, a drama played out among mysterious alien forces which never conduce to a proper 'tragic' destiny. The protagonist, king or courtier, is a figure of saturnine and vacillating temperament, acted upon by humours which he can neither understand nor control. The action of the *Trauerspiel* (like that of a Webster or Tourneur revenge-play) is a business of absurdly distorted motives and plans turned back upon their inventors' heads. It is, Benjamin argues, a totally 'non-Aristotelian' form of drama, though not in the radical Brechtian sense which Benjamin had yet to encounter. *Trauerspiel* is played out under the dark auspices of a stoic philosophy which denies the transcendent unifying focus of a tragic catharsis. It enacts the apparently senseless sufferings of a secular world unredeemed by any saving or transformative vision.

Benjamin's thesis was more than an exercise in arcane scholarly research. It carries along with it a whole philosophy of language, history and thought, the significance of which Benjamin expounds in his 'Epistemo-critical prologue'. His writing here is deliberately dense and resistant to summary explanation. It turns on the distinction between 'knowledge' and 'truth', which Benjamin sees as two different orders of representation, the one amenable to systematic statement and theory, the other belonging to a realm of somehow self-evident (and hence inexplicable) prior understanding. As Benjamin expresses it:

> Truth, bodied forth in the dance of represented ideas, resists being projected, by whatever means, into the realm of knowledge. Knowledge is possession ... for the thing possessed, representation is secondary; it does not have prior existence as something representing itself. But the opposite holds good of truth. For knowledge, method is a way of acquiring its object – even by creating it in the consciousness; for truth it is self-representation, and is therefore immanent in it as form.[18]

In their tortuous, disjunct style of construction these sentences enact the dilemma which Benjamin finds at the heart of all aesthetic discourse. Where 'knowledge' creates a regulative sequence of orderly, self-possessed reasoning, 'truth' demands a disjunctive style which has to hold out against the lures of logical and grammatical entailment. 'The writer', as Benjamin says, 'must stop and restart with every new sentence.'

This rejection of philosophy as a systematic edifice, in favour of a pared-down or aphoristic style, was of course nothing new in the history of philosophic thought. Nietzsche and Kierkegaard had reacted against Hegel for much the same reason, though to very different ends. Benjamin's distinction between 'truth' and 'knowledge' also finds a parallel in Wittgenstein's assertion that 'what can be shown cannot be said'; a consequence of his believing, like Benjamin, that certain propositional forms stood in a privileged relation to truth, irreducible to further analysis. For Wittgenstein this meant an end to pointless philosophical chatter. 'Whereof one cannot speak, thereof should one remain silent.' For Benjamin, on the contrary, it leads into a labyrinth of endlessly displaced allegorical meanings which yield to the interpreter's melancholy art without hope of any final, self-assured significance.

Such is the 'bottomless pit of contemplation' which Benjamin discovers in his seventeenth-century texts. He associates the ethos of *Trauerspiel* with the baroque habit of compiling emblem-books and other such 'stock requisites of gloomy spectacle'. Images take on a deathly stillness, a stark materiality of meaning which resists interpretation except by a kind of arbitrary shuffling and juxtaposition. The *Faustus* theme of arcane and dangerous knowledge goes along with a helpless sense of the infinite allegorical permutations opened up when meaning is deprived of any 'transcendental' ground. Such knowledge is the constant burden of *Trauerspiel* and baroque allegory in general:

> Tirelessly transforming, interpreting and deepening, it rings the changes on its images ... the throne room is transformed into the dungeon, the pleasure-chamber into a tomb, the crown into a wreath of bloody cypress.[19]

This is the Gnostic vision of evil, a world in which souls are ensnared by the emblems of mortality, and knowledge bound up with demonic intimations of a godless material universe. The 'theology of evil' in baroque drama is connected with a bad infinity of meaning, an abysmal regress of allegory where the interpreter must fear to tread.

It is this dimension of *Trauerspiel* which holds up a mirror to Benjamin's tortuous meditations on language and meaning. The ideas put forward in his Prologue are fleshed out in the emblems and characters of baroque imagination, their significance vividly captured in Benjamin's prose. When he writes of the Faustian 'polymath' as a figure beset by all the dangers of secular

knowledge, it is clearly Benjamin's own situation – his predicament as critic-philosopher – which lights up these fragments of
historical memory. For the stoic-contemplative protagonist of
Trauerspiel, as indeed for his present-day interpreter,

> something can take on allegorical form only if the man
> possesses knowledge. But on the other hand, if contempla-
> tion is not so much patiently devoted to truth, as uncon-
> ditionally and compulsively, in direct meditation, bent on
> absolute knowledge, then it is eluded by things, in the
> simplicity of their essence, and they lie before it as enigmatic
> allegorical references, they continue to be dust.[20]

The imagery of dust, ruins and physical catastrophe runs
through Benjamin's work like an obsessive motif. It is linked to
his catastrophist idea of historical 'progress' as a piling-up of
endless losses and disasters, unredeemable unless by the spark
of recognition which flashes across time. Allegory stands in the
same relation to interpretative thought as ruins to the edifice of
Hegelian historicism. In both cases it is Benjamin's conviction
that hope can only survive through a chastening awareness of
the forces massed against it, a thwarting of premature meanings
and ideals.

IV

Eagleton's book is a Marxist intervention, a strategic effort to
capture Benjamin's thought before the forces of reaction can
blunt its revolutionary impact. Far from disabling his argument
this squares with Benjamin's own acute sense of the shifting and
provisional character of texts, their openness to new 'constella-
tions' of meaning. On the other hand Eagleton is far from
endorsing the kind of easygoing relativist tolerance which
would find a place for the Marxist reading among other, equally
valid modes of approach. The thrust of his argument is to drive
a wedge between Benjamin's revolutionary thought (however
elusive its formulations) and any account which enlists it in the
service of a merely 'textual' radicalism.

There is no doubting Benjamin's appeal to the current deconstructors, who have already produced some intricate rhetorical
readings of his texts.[21] The *Trauerspiel* book is uncannily

prescient of themes which have come to preoccupy critical discussion under Derrida's influence. Deconstruction is aimed at dismantling the metaphysical presuppositions which it finds deeply entrenched in the history of western philosophy and literature. It seeks to reveal the 'logocentric' bias which subjugates writing to speech, the latter conceived as a self-present plenitude of meaning which alone guarantees the authenticity of language. Deconstruction, as we have seen, sets out to reverse this prejudice, to show how metaphors of writing and textual inscription disrupt every attempt to preserve the metaphysics of presence. From Plato to Saussure, the privileged status of speech is linked with a desire to represent language as coinciding with knowledge and experience in a pure, unmediated act of consciousness. From this point of view writing can only appear as a secondary, derived or merely 'parasitical' mode of signification, as opposed to the direct self-present truth of speech.[22]

The speech/writing opposition thus becomes the pivot upon which revolve all the great philosophical questions of language, meaning and truth. As Derrida shows, these controversies are concerned not so much with the literal sense of 'writing' (graphic inscription), as with the figural dimension where meanings are wrenched away from origin by the disseminating play of language itself. Speech is always already inhabited by structures of signification which nowhere coincide with a speaker's 'original' intent. Writing is in this sense a synecdoche for all those slippages and detours of meaning where linguistic figuration comes into play. It threatens philosophy by drawing attention to the non-self-identical character of thought in general, the extent to which writing disrupts the illusion of a perfect reciprocity between signifier and signified. Deconstruction thus suspends all traditional concepts of meaning. It operates instead with paradoxical key-terms (like Derrida's *differance*) which insist on the freeplay of language and on their own irreducibly graphic character.

It is not hard to see how these ideas make contact with Benjamin's thinking on language and aesthetics. Deconstruction is squarely opposed, like the *Trauerspiel* study, to any philosophy of interpretation which seeks out meaning as an ultimate or 'transcendental' signified. The preference for allegory over symbol, as more faithfully reflecting the condition of interpretative thought, is likewise common to Benjamin and the current deconstructors. This is a constant preoccupation of Paul de Man's criticism. He sees the aesthetics of Romantic and Modernist poetry as based upon a rhetoric of self-deception, one which holds out the image of a perfect, transparent communing between mind and nature, while achieving that effect by what amount to surreptitious means. De Man pursues the figurative gaps and elisions of meaning by which symbol and metaphor – the touchstones of Romantic transcendence – are deconstructed into chains of metonymic detail. Idealist philosophies are shown to rest on a blindness to their own rhetorical working, a motive which substitutes the dream of unified perception for the discrete particulars of apprehended meaning.[23]

The same applies to those organicist theories of criticism which, as de Man argues, mistake their own image of interpretative wholeness and integrity for that of the work itself. Form is the product of a 'dialectical interplay' between text and critical presupposition. This is how de Man deconstructs the American formalist (or New Critical) aesthetic:

> Because such delicate and patient attention was paid to the reading of forms, the critic pragmatically entered into the hermeneutic circle of interpretation, mistaking it for the organic circularity of natural processes.[24]

For de Man such blind-spots in the rhetoric of poetry and criticism are sources of insight at a higher dialectical (or deconstructionist) level. Yet he often seems to regard them – especially where Symbolist aesthetics are concerned – as a rhetoric of mystification amounting to sheer bad faith.

In this he concurs with Benjamin, likewise promoting 'allegory' over 'symbol' as a means of coming to terms with the inbuilt limitations of interpretative thought. Benjamin approaches the *Trauerspiel* as a form to be rescued from the version of literary history spawned by Romantic and Symbolist creeds of aesthetic transcendence. He castigates Symbolism as the 'resplendent but ultimately non-committal knowledge of an absolute'. Romanticism has promoted a false aesthetic of the symbol which 'insists on the indivisible unity of form and content', yet fails through its lack of 'dialectical rigour' to 'do justice to content in formal analysis and to form in the aesthetics of content'.[25]

This is the crux of Benjamin's quarrel with Romanticism. Where the aesthetics of the symbol leads to a premature and abortive idealization, allegory entails a very different habit of thought, one which respects the paradoxical limits of all interpretation. Its 'eccentric and dialectic process', in Benjamin's words, is one which finds no place for the 'harmonious inwardness' of meaning, since its visible signs are so insistently *there* on the surface and resist the mystique of Romantic transcendence. In a passage which strikingly anticipates Derrida, Benjamin discusses Schopenhauer's attitude to allegory and *writing* as equivalent modes of debased (because conventional or arbitrary) meaning. Just as writing betrays the self-presence of speech into the fragments of an alien, materialized text, so allegory threatens the Symbolist ideal of aesthetic wholeness and vision. *Trauerspiel* is the very enactment of this fall into the scattered emblems of a strange, unintelligible meaning:

> The mournful has the feeling that it is known comprehensively by the unknowable. To be named – even if the name-giver is god-like and saintly – perhaps always brings with it a presentiment of mourning. But how much more so not to be named, to be read uncertainly by the allegorist, and to have become highly significant only thanks to him.[26]

It is a 'mournful' condition but, as Benjamin argues, one which the interpreter cannot escape without bad faith or mystification.

Eagleton reserves his fiercest polemics for what he sees as the tactics of political evasion promoted by the Yale deconstructors. Theirs is a form of 'ultra-left' radicalism, a self-destructive enterprise bent upon showing that no possible discourse (its own included) can escape the 'logocentric' tyranny of western metaphysics. Political questions disappear from view while texts are relentlessly quizzed to reveal the tell-tale gaps and *aporiai* of meaning where deconstruction can obtain a hold. If language is deluded at source in the idea that it can represent *any* kind of truth without thereby falling into traps of its own metaphysical engendering, then clearly there is no good reason for choosing one political language over another, since both must ultimately exhibit the same rhetorical blindness. Eagleton compares deconstruction with the suicidal bomb-carrying anarchist professor in Conrad's *The Secret Agent*. The Yale critics dream of some 'unutterably radical' enterprise which would 'blow a black hole in the whole set-up and forcibly induce its self-transcendence into some condition beyond all current discourse'.[27] This is the only recourse available to thought when ideology is conceived, not in terms of specific historical formations, but as a kind of aboriginal swerve from grace within language itself, a delusion operative (as Eagleton puts it) 'all the way from Plato to NATO'.

Benjamin's texts thus remain a battle-ground of rival interpretative strategies. Up to now the main issues have been fought between Marxists on the one hand, anxious to ignore the utopian-visionary aspect of Benjamin's thinking, and those like Gershom Scholem who treat his Marxist inclinations as merely the result of Brecht's pernicious influence. Eagleton's book marks a definite shift of position in response to new kinds of challenge on the non-Marxist front. He discovers the revolutionary potential of Benjamin's texts precisely in their power to disconcert more rigid or positivist conceptions of Marxist criticism. Benjamin's melancholy vision of historical 'progress', his brooding on the emblematic detritus of *Trauerspiel*, could hardly be further removed from the mainstream of Marxist-materialist thought. His messianic images of time redeemed – of history transfigured in the instant of divine intervention – are equally remote from any kind of secular enlightenment. For Eagleton, these themes are not to be ignored or 'dialectically' transumed, but demand a commensurate effort of mind on the interpreter's part. 'The intensity with which Benjamin lived this aporia distinguishes him just as much from the sanguine teleology of a Lukács as it does from the occasional facile philistinism of a Brecht.'[28]

Deconstruction is the enemy still to be resisted when Marxism has reached this unlikely accord with the mystical elements in Benjamin's thought. That Eagleton should use the term 'aporia' – invoking the Aristotelian rhetoric of deconstruction even while denouncing its effects – is evidence of the struggle being waged at close quarters by these two most advanced and antagonistic forms of modern critical consciousness. It is also a reflection of Benjamin's belief, expressed most forcefully in the *Trauerspiel* book: that meaning eludes the consistency of knowledge and resides in its eccentric details and discrepancies. 'In the ruins of great buildings the idea of the plan speaks more impressively than in lesser buildings, however well preserved they are.'[29] It is ironic that Benjamin's texts have provoked such intense possessive rivalry among the system-building architects of present-day critical theory.

Benjamin's writings, I have argued, have this much in common with the textual activity of deconstruction. They point to the crucial blind-spot of Romantic epistemology: its deluded overreaching of language and sense in quest of some transcendent, self-sustained vision irreducible to mere linguistic signs. In Chapter 6 I pursue this connection by examining an established classic of Romantic scholarship, J. Livingston Lowes' *The Road to Xanadu*. Few works could offer more striking evidence of the twists and detours, the varieties of roundabout textual alibi, engendered in post-Romantic critical discourse. And at the root of this condition, I shall argue, are the issues of language and representation as waged since Kant between empiricist and idealist philosophies of mind. Suspended undecidably between two traditions, two rival accountings for language and thought, Lowes' text can only repeat their difference through constantly reduplicated narratives of its own critical quest. This generative logic of paradox and displacement is that which deconstruction finds at work in the discourse of Romantic poetry and criticism.

6

Forked paths to Xanadu: parables of reading in Livingston Lowes

It is almost sixty years since A. O. J. Lovejoy published his influential essay 'On the discrimination of Romanticisms'.[1] Scholars have debated the claims of that essay, some of them wishing to qualify its pluralist outlook in the interest of preserving some workable sense of 'the Romantic' as a broad generic concept, if not as a unitary phenomenon. But on the whole – as usual with scholarly endeavour – the trend has been to multiply distinctions and cast doubt on tidy, panoptic generalizations. Literary critics and theorists have moved in what seems an opposite direction. Perhaps the most notable feature of current (post-structuralist) critical writing is the way it has restored the Romantics to an intellectual dignity and central importance denied them by T. S. Eliot and his academic followers. Critics like Geoffrey Hartman and Paul de Man have rejected not only the privileged 'tradition' of Eliot's creating, but the entire epistemology of language, truth and logic which underlay that tradition.[2] What Eliot famously disliked about the Romantics was their overreaching of the poet's proper interests, their straining beyond the bounds of disciplined thought toward a realm of transcendent knowledge which could only – for Eliot – amount to a drastic, even blasphemous confusion of ends.[3] For the current deconstructors it is precisely this sense of intellectual strain – of language and logic pressed up against their limits – which identifies and paradoxically validates the 'rhetoric of Romanticism'.

Deconstruction is irreducible to method or technique, its 'theory' resistant to any kind of summary description. These critics' conclusions are reached through a strenuous wrestling with the text, a style of close reading very different from the way in which the 'old' New Criticism, in its academic heyday, sought out structures of 'irony' or 'paradox' to back up its claims for the privileged autonomy of poetic language. The interpreter, for his part, respected that autonomy by preserving a due sense of the *difference* – unbridgeable and absolute – between poetry and criticism. At most he might reflect uneasily – like Allen Tate and R. P. Blackmur in speculative vein – on the tensions and frustrations involved in this policing of ontological bounds.[4] Among the deconstructors these tensions have arrived at the point of a full-scale reversal (some would say a breakdown) of the disciplined relation between 'text' and 'commentary'. This change has taken various forms, stylistic and philosophical. In Geoffrey Hartman it has produced an agonistic style of inter-pretative auto-critique, a probing of the self-conscious motives and drives which enter increasingly to baffle and complicate the critic's response to the text.[5] With Paul de Man these com-plexities are argued through to the point of an ultimate 'un-decidability' which infects all forms of discourse, philosophy and criticism included. Literary texts represent for de Man at once the most 'rigorous' and the most 'unreliable' source of knowledge, 'rigorous' precisely to the degree that they question and subvert any straightforward idea of textual logic or veracity.[6]

I have written at length elsewhere about the consequences of deconstruction and its effect on the interpreter's self-image *vis-à-vis* the text.[7] This chapter is more concerned with its specific bearings on the language and epistemological claims of Romantic poetry. The paradox here is that deconstruction values the achievements of Romanticism precisely in so far as they signally *fail* to make good their own highest promise. This exemplary failure is not, as Eliot argued, a result of woolly-mindedness or mere rhetorical afflatus. It is the upshot of language forced to the limit of self-critical reflection on its own nature and genesis. The 'rigorous unreliability' of language is thus laid bare as a salutary lesson for criticism and philosophy alike. Where the Romantics typically overreach themselves – as

in aiming for a pure, unmediated vision, a perfect correspondence between idea, language and reality – their failure is a
heightened and dramatized version of the problems which beset
all thought. To deconstruct the Romantic ideology is not to
assume some higher dialectical ground from which to trace the
curious persistence of a local and corrigible error. Rather, it is to
recognize that any form of discourse, once alerted to its own
paradoxical condition, cannot do more than self-critically rehearse the *necessary delusions* which produce and sustain it. Thus
de Man sees Nietzsche as having forced upon philosophy the
prospect of a hard-earned scepticism which 'advocates the use
of epistemologically rigorous methods as the only possible
means to reflect on the limitations of those methods'.[8] In this
respect Nietzsche is the active antithesis – but also the accom-
plice – of those poet-philosophers like Coleridge and Goethe
whose metaphors de Man deconstructs as signs of a textual
will-to-power beyond reach of actual attainment.

To summarize very simply, there are three main grounds on
which deconstruction engages and subverts the rhetoric of
Romanticism:

1 The claims of metaphor and symbol – most privileged of
   Romantic tropes – are shown to decompose, on closer
   reading, into chains of *metonymic* or causal-associative detail. This produces:
2 a breakdown in the means of transcending the ontological
   divide, the dualism of subject and object, inward and
   outward experience, which Romantic metaphor strove to
   overcome. And, following from this:
3 it is argued that Romantic discourse ceaselessly covers its
   own rhetorical tracks, passing off as Symbol (or self-
   sufficient metaphor) those passages which in the end come
   down to a species of *allegory*, or meaning artificially contrived and sustained.

Deconstruction thus amounts to a resolute critique of the central
motivating impulse in Romantic poetics: the desire to reduce
multiplicity to unity, or time (succession) to an instant of
luminous, all-embracing vision. In de Man this produces an
insistent, almost obsessive concern to demystify the figurative
power which otherwise blinds a 'naïve' reading to the covert

metaphysics vested in Romantic metaphor. Acquiescence in this power becomes, for de Man, virtually a species of critical bad faith. There may be 'no end to what tropes can get away with',[9] but thought is not thereby absolved from seeing through the means of its own too-willing deception.

De Man's is a rigorous and self-denying ordinance, a pyrrhic critique always on the verge of defeating its own provisional insights. Geoffrey Hartman is more frankly exuberant in his sense of the prospects opened up by this new dynamic interplay between literature and the ruses of interpretative thought. Once the critic despairs – as despair he must – of attaining the 'unmediated vision', the unimpeded merging of mind and nature held out by Romantic metaphor, he is then set free to explore the endless complexities of meaning and textual figuration. Criticism celebrates a new-found autonomy which brings it out pretty much on a level with the psychic drama of doubt and self-division which Romantic poetry strives to articulate. The pleasures of naïve empathy are a world well lost, Hartman implies, if their elusiveness can conjure such subtle satisfactions of interpretative theory. 'I think that is where we are now. We have entered an age which can challenge even the priority of literary to literary-critical texts.'[10] For all his professed misgivings ('things get mixed up in this jittery situation'), Hartman can scarcely disguise the vertiginous excitement it affords. Interpretation is henceforth an activity of *writing*, not to be downgraded by comparison with 'primary' texts which themselves perforce witness their failure to achieve an unmediated vision beyond grasp of language or thought.

This is why the texts of Romanticism – poems and commentaries alike – exert such a special fascination for the current deconstructors. The Romantic ideal is a form of indissoluble fusion between language and reality, mind and object, such that all extraneous detail falls away in the moment of achieved communion. Wordsworth's poetry is a constant attempt to bend syntax, logic and narrative progression to the point where mind could identify with nature in the sense of 'one life, within me and abroad'. Yet such moments can only be achieved through a build-up of figural and narrative devices which subtly work to undermine the claim to this hypostatic union. The effect is yet more pronounced in those commentaries and critiques which the Romantics provided by way of explaining their own poetic aims. Coleridge offers some instructive examples. His notorious attempt to *explain* 'Kubla Khan' – to extenuate its visionary strangeness by spinning a narrative account of the circumstances which surrounded its writing – constitutes in itself a kind of demystifying tactic.[11] Like Shelley's 'Ozymandias', the poem comes close to the Romantic ideal of a symbolic world-out-of-time, a spatialized projection of metaphor and myth unhampered by accidents of circumstance or genesis. Yet Coleridge himself set a pattern for future interpreters by stepping down – somewhat embarrassed – from the heights of prophetic inspiration, and offering his prosy account of the dream interrupted by workaday business. The circumstantial reasons for this narrative contrivance – the role played by opium and Coleridge's guilt on that score – are of no great relevance here. What signifies is the poet's strange compulsion to *deconstruct* into temporal and contingent terms a poem which seemed set fair to achieve the looked-for Romantic state of transcendent apprehension.

Another famous crux of Coleridgean thought occurs in Chapter XIII of *Biographia Literaria*, where the argument is abruptly cut short by yet another item of intrusive circumstance, namely the letter from 'a friend' piously enjoining Coleridge not to continue his abstruse researches.[12] The genuineness of the pretext, or the exact nature of Coleridge's scruples, are again not the main points at issue here. As with 'Kubla Khan', it happens that at this stage in his argument Coleridge the philosopher is preparing to formulate the ultimate statement – or crowning synthesis – of his previous oblique remarks on the nature of Imagination. In short, the *Biographia* is moving toward a discursive or philosophic treatment of the issues raised in tantalizing form by the fragmentary 'Kubla Khan'. Thought seems poised to create a transcendent and all-embracing image of its own activity, a synthesis of subject and object such as to abolish all need for the props and mediations of conventional discourse. But to achieve such ecstatic union would mean discarding the very forms of intelligible argument, dependent as these are on predicative structures and on *sequence*, or unfolding implication, as opposed to the sheer simultaneous grasp afforded (purportedly) by pure Imagination. The very attempt to describe such a faculty could only end by listing its attributes, reducing its operations to a matter of mechanical succession, and thus deconstructing the source of all metaphor – the grounding metaphor itself – into a series of discrete and contingent metonymies.

De Man, in his essay 'The rhetoric of temporality', shows with great precision how this problem affects many texts of the major Romantics, Coleridge included:

> Starting out from the assumed superiority of the symbol in terms of organic substantiality, we end up with a description of figural language as translucence, a description in which the distinction between allegory and symbol has become of secondary importance.[13]

Allegory of course belongs to a temporal dimension, a narrative sequence, while the language of Symbolism takes effect – or, as de Man would argue, *fails* to take effect – in a timeless moment of transcendent unified perception. The discrete, serial character of allegory is thus reflected in those curious trumped-up narrative excuses which Coleridge hits upon to justify or circumvent his own argumentative quandaries. The quest for an originating metaphor of thought becomes sidetracked or betrayed into parables and fictions which more or less cunningly evade the issue. And indeed, as we shall see, such episodes mark not only the founding texts of Romantic tradition, but also the history of subsequent attempts to come to terms with them.

II

J. Livingston Lowes' *The Road to Xanadu* is not, on the face of it, a work of 'philosophical' criticism.[14] It is regarded – rightly enough – as a monument of source-hunting scholarship, a fantastic voyage (to adopt Lowes' own favourite metaphor) through the uncharted seas of Coleridge's reading in the period which produced 'The Ancient Mariner' and 'Kubla Khan'. The book is perhaps sufficiently well-known to require no lengthy description here. Its mass of documentary evidence – from travellers' tales, scientific treatises, histories and records of every kind, factual and fictive – would seem to place it squarely in the camp of historical-comparative scholarship. Lowes himself is quick to disclaim any interest in following out the speculative bias of Coleridge's mind. The questions raised in Chapters XII and XIII of *Biographia Literaria* belong, he argues, to 'the history of critical opinion', while his own chief concern is with 'a study of the imaginative processes themselves'. And, more outspokenly:

> I cannot but think that Coleridge's most precious contribution to our understanding of the imagination lies, not in his metaphysical lucubrations on it after it was lost, but in the implications of his practice while he yet possessed the power.[15]

True to his word, Lowes avoids any direct critical engagement with the speculative side of Coleridge's thought, merely picking up the occasional hint or distinction when it touches on the workings of associative memory which Lowes is determined to uncover.

One cannot but be struck by this principled disregard of the Copernican upheaval which overtook Coleridge with his reading of Kant, and which caused his abandonment of Locke, Hartley and the British empiricist tradition. Of course it must be taken into account that Lowes' book was published in 1927, some decades before Wellek and others set about revealing the full effect of Kant's transcendental critique on Coleridge's nascent philosophy of mind. There is also the seemingly knock-down argument that Coleridge commenced his serious studies of German metaphysics in the early years of the nineteenth century, while 'Kubla Khan' and 'The Ancient Mariner' date from his poetic high-point of the late 1790s. Hence Lowes' confident assumption that the poems were unaffected by the subsequent 'metaphysical lucubrations'. But this is to ignore a number of complicating factors. Coleridge was clearly exposed to the new German current of ideas long before he undertook their systematic study. Moreover, as D. M. MacKinnon argues in a recent essay on Coleridge and Kant, 'it may well be that he received the work of the German philosophers . . . as seeming to contain answers to questions in the philosophy of mind posed to him by his experience as a poet.'[16]

At any rate it is fair to remark on the singular avoidance of philosophic themes in Lowes' reconstruction of the poet's psychology and habits of mind. His enormous documentary detective-work in other directions makes it all the more difficult not to suspect a certain systematic *blindness* in Lowes' great project. Three possible reasons suggest themselves. Firstly, there is the fact that Lowes set out to write what amounted to a Lockean or Hartleian account of Coleridge's mental workings. The philosophy of this – so far as it needs one – comes down to an unreconstructed blend of associationist images and metaphors. (The 'hooked atoms' of Epicurus are Lowes' most frequent analogical recourse in describing the interanimation of ideas.) Secondly, his book is cast in narrative or diegetic form, reflecting on the one hand Lowes' own detective-work in piecing his evidence together, and on the other – supposedly – the corresponding growth or psychological genesis of Coleridge's poems. It may be relevant at this point to recall what de Man has to say about the 'rhetoric of temporality' and its inbuilt resistance to the totalizing claims of any transcendent metaphysic or epistemology. Thirdly, it is clear that Lowes was writing out of the American pragmatist tradition, suspicious of abstract philosophic systems and strongly inclined toward a materialist outlook in matters of psychology. William James is quoted on several occasions, unlike Kant whose one brief appearance is in a footnote of minimal importance. There is, in short, a marked subjugation of everything pertaining to Romantic idealist philosophy, and an opposite stress on the aspects of mental *process* – conceived in materialist terms – which underlie the poems' imagery and language.

These points may seem less than germane when set against the splendidly manifold scenery of Lowes' mental voyage. And indeed they would be if it were not for the passages of felt misgiving where Lowes stops to question the deeper implications of his method. These doubts have to do with the conflict, as Lowes perceives it, between poetic creativity and the kind of mechanical-associative process which his findings seem to indicate. At several points he reverts uneasily to Coleridge's cardinal distinction between 'fancy' and 'imagination', mostly with the purpose of denying its ultimate validity, or arguing for a relativized scale of difference. The problem, of course, is that Lowes' account of the poems makes them sound very much like products of 'fancy', nonpareil examples of the kind (he would argue) but finally resolvable, through patient exploration, to a process of associative linkage. Lowes has a comforting footnote which cites the opinion of Lascelles Abercrombie: 'fancy is nothing but a degree of imagination; and the degree of it concerns, not the quality of the imagery, but the quality and force of the emotion symbolized by the imagery.'[17] But the saving vagueness of this and formulations like it – of which Lowes provides many examples – does little to relieve the sense of philosophic unease.

What seems to be enacted here is the interpreter's unwilling compulsion to *repeat*, in his own quest for meaning, the blind-spots and paradoxes engendered by the texts he interprets. We have seen how Coleridge found himself constrained to circumvent the problems of his own idealist metaphysic by constructing various kinds of narrative alibi through which to represent them as a species of private case-history. Lowes confronts the opposite face of this dilemma. His method is firmly committed to the narrative mode of exposition, based on the foregone assumption that Coleridge's poems can be traced back to origin through a process of patiently unpacking their manifold allusions. In this respect Lowes starts out pre-convinced of the case which a critic like de Man seeks to establish through the rigours of deconstruction. 'Imagination' is progressively decomposed into the elements of 'fancy'. The ideology of Symbol and Metaphor – the 'unmediated vision' of Romantic aspriation – is in both cases reduced to a matter of discrete and piecemeal perception. Yet Lowes cannot help but counterpoint his text with passages of markedly idealizing metaphor and imagery which betray the continuing hold of Romantic ideology:

> I have no desire to explain away the unexplainable, and behind the discoverable processes through which beauty is created ... is and will always be something inscrutable, which no analysis can reach – or harm.[18]

The Road to Xanadu contains many such examples of anxious reassurance, to readers and author alike. It also comes up with a variety of metaphors – often incongruously mixed – by way of trying to reconcile the 'organic' and the 'mechanical', 'imagination' and 'fancy', creativity and mere vivid memory.

One example may suffice. Lowes takes up a passage from Epicetus, using the simile of a game of dice as a means of presenting the issues of freewill and necessity. He adapts the metaphor, predictably enough, to deal with the conflict of commitments present in his own critical method. It is 'the subliminal ego' which throws up the various chance combinations, 'as the throng of sleeping images, at this call or that, move toward the light'. But this element of chance once accepted, something else takes over: 'the shaping spirit of imagination conceives and masterfully carries out the strategy of the game.'[19] In fact Lowes' metaphor shifts mid-argument from Epicetus' dice to a game of *cards*, no doubt because this lends more conviction to the idea of 'conceiving a strategy' to regulate the workings of chance. All the same, it does not take a Wittgensteinian philosopher to see how the analogy comes under strain as soon as game-playing *rules* are added to the basic determinist picture. 'Strategy' remains a viable term, but 'the shaping spirit of imagination' sounds very much like creating the rules as the game goes along.

It may seem perverse to press so hard on a passing illustrative metaphor. But the same thing occurs, in a great variety of figurative guises, on almost every page of Lowes' text. The effect is to situate his argument on a shifting metaphorical ground where *method* can perform its demythologizing work, while *rhetoric* – of a vaguely idealizing nature – steps in to save poetic appearances. The card-playing analogy gives way within a paragraph to the following, more high-toned, passage: 'There still remains the architectonic imagination, moving, *sua sponte*, among the scattered fragments, and discerning, latent in their confusion, the pattern of a whole.'[20] This romanticized Kantian reflection is distinctly at odds with the actual workings of Lowes' associative method. It derives, quite plainly, from the later Coleridgean philosophy, those enfeebled 'metaphysical lucubrations' which Lowes elsewhere sets aside as inimical to a true understanding of the poetry. There is a deep-rooted conflict, in short, between the materialist-associative psychology which Lowes adopts for all practical purposes, and the strain of idealist philosophy which his arguments can never entirely subdue.

This conflict produces some striking forms of thematic displacement, or figural reworking, in Lowes' train of thought. Like Coleridge, he tends to shift the burden of argument onto parables or anecdotes from his own past experience whenever the demands of explanatory method come up against those of creative autonomy. These episodes are intended to illuminate, by suggestively reliving, the process of imaginative fusion which went into the making of Coleridge's poems. Most often they involve a dream-state or condition of suspended conscious control where elements from Lowes' own reading are freed to coalesce into a virtual *recreation* of the lines or stanzas involved. The status of these anecdotes, whether 'genuine' or fictitious, and the extent to which they serve as retroactive pretexts for Lowes' critical approach, can only be matter for speculation. As with Freudian analysis, the meaning of dreams may often be projected back into them not only by the patient's waking mind, but by the analyst in search of significant data. An element of *post hoc* rationalization marks the very discourse of interpretative reason.

In Lowes' case, however, the ambiguities are multiplied by the fact that 'Kubla Khan' already comes equipped with a framing dream-narrative purporting to interpret its psychological genesis. Lowes seems compelled to repeat the strange gesture – whatever its confusedly extenuating motive – which produced the circumstantial trappings of Coleridge's dream. Perhaps it is the case – as certain critics have argued – that interpretation is always somehow fated to act out the same alternation of blindness and insight as punctuates the literary text. Christine Brooke-Rose has made the point to good effect in her recent reading of various critics on Henry James' *The Turn of the Screw*. 'The critics reproduce the very tendencies they so often note in the governess: omission; assertion; elaboration; lying even (or, when the critics do so, let us call it error).'[21] Barbara Johnson arrives at a similar conclusion in reflecting on the constant errors and blind-spots to which all interpretation is prone. Criticism, she writes, is 'often the straight man whose precarious rectitude and hidden risibility, passion, and pathos are precisely what literature has somehow already foreseen'.[22] Lowes' 'wild night of fantastic dreams' – leading up to the vicarious recreation of 'Kubla Khan' – is a case of retrojection so frankly acknowledged as to seem beyond need of deconstructive treatment. In another sense, however, it stands to his normal (or 'waking') critical procedures as a species of alibi, a means of evading their awkwardly reductive implications.

The details are presented with some care for authenticity and credible truth. (A footnote insists that 'the dream was set down at once', and that Lowes is not 'relying on later memory'.) Its events are indeed lucidly described, so much so – and with such pointed reference both to the poem and to Lowes' present business of interpreting – that dream and critical commentary can hardly be distinguished.

> After I had spent some time in taking 'Kubla Khan' out of a clothes basket in successive layers like stiff and freshly laundered shirts, the dream abruptly shifted from its impish travesty of my waking efforts to a vision so lucidly clear that after the lapse of five years, as I write, it is as fresh as when I actually saw it.[23]

What follows is a catalogue of visual detail ('the sunny dome', 'the deep romantic chasm', 'the sacred river') which sedulously mimes and elaborates the poem's descriptive progress. It is capped by the claim that 'not the faintest hint of what I saw had ever entered into any conscious visualization of the setting.'

The dream-logic of this narrative is worthy of remark on several counts. The 'successive layers' like 'stiff laundered shirts' suggest very strongly the reductive, mechanistic philosophy which Lowes half-suspects in his own scholarly dealings with the poem. And in passing from this to the visionary sweep of its subsequent details, the passage contrives to effect independently that radical shift, or transcendent apprehension, which Lowes refuses to countenance in philosophic terms. The limits of his applied psychology can only be overcome by literally *rewriting* 'Kubla Khan' at the level of displaced surrogate experience provided by the dream-narrative. Its progression is a veritable 'allegory of reading', to adopt de Man's terminology. That is, it unfolds through a sequence of interpretative moves which both strain toward a sense of ultimate, inward understanding and at the same time confess – by their narrative contrivance – the impossible nature of any such achievement.

III

'Behind the poem as a poem stands the dream as a dream' writes Lowes, referring in this case to Coleridge's 'original' dream. His intention is clearly to *authenticate* the poem by insisting on its roots in a region of the poet's most intimate and vivid pre-conscious experience. But this appeal misses the mark, as Lowes' own argument is implicitly forced to concede. The two dream-narratives enter into a shuttling relationship and interchange of detail which produce an uncanny merging, each with the other and *both* with the poem that stands to them either as product or pretext. It was precisely this pattern of 'uncanny' (*unheimlich*) repetition which Freud came to recognize in the structures of unconscious discourse.[24] He also remarked that they possessed, as it were, a power of metaphorical contagion, passing from patient to analyst – or from dream to waking explanation – through relays of figural displacement which reason seemed powerless to contain or control. Theory itself was 'uncannily' pre-empted by metaphors beyond its rational grasp.

Neil Hertz has recently addressed these problems in a fine deconstructionist reading of Freud's late essay on the repetition-complex. He shows how the essay becomes entangled with a strange variety of themes – 'a work of fiction, a psychoanalytic account of its structure, the formulation of a metapsychological theory, some biographical anecdotes' – and how it finally runs up against the limiting paradox of all narrative explanations. As Hertz puts it, the 'repetition complex'

> may then have seemed to its discoverer to have taken on an uncanny life of its own; indeed, the very uncertainty as to whether it was the force 'itself' or its theoretical formulation that was claiming attention would contribute to the effect of strangeness.[25]

This juncture of themes has an obvious bearing on Lowes' attempt to reconstruct the genesis of Coleridge's poems. It suggests, for one thing, how that arch-Romantic topos – the problematic of origins – works to create a potentially endless series of allegories, narratives and other such surrogate forms of thematic repetition. The further Lowes pushes back toward the 'origin' of Coleridge's vision, the more his language is forced to reveal its unavailability to *any* kind of present reconstruction.

'Kubla Khan' is thus deprived even of its status as a text holding out some promise of understanding through the words and images which actually compose it. The mystique of origins gives way to the lure of dreams, and substitutes a secondary storytelling interest for the problems of interpreting the poem. The best that Lowes can hope for, he writes, is to aid the reader in conjuring up:

> some semblance of that irretrievable vision which was neither the several images that flashed up from oblivion to frame it, nor yet the imperishably lovely words which veil it, as they reveal it, to our eyes.[26]

High-flown phraseology apart, this passage enacts the twofold dilemma which everywhere confronts Lowes' critical method. It confesses that the poem cannot be conceived as simply the sum of its constitutive parts as rescued from oblivion by Lowes' patient source-hunting scholarship. Associationist psychology yields to the lure of transcendental aesthetics. At the same time it fixes an insuperable gulf between the poem itself and the supposed 'original' dream which the poem's imagery can only 'reveal' by 'veiling' its visionary sources.

Lowes' entire approach depends, as we have seen, on his electing to ignore or repress the idealizing strain of Romantic metaphysics. He effectively *reverses* the chapter of intellectual history which witnessed the shift from empiricist to idealist thinking, not only in Coleridge's prototype case but in the great majority of subsequent attempts to grasp the workings of Romantic thought. The claims and problems of epistemology are here rejected in favour of a resolutely materialist and psycho-biographical approach. To this extent, it might be argued, Lowes gives voice to something like the modern hermeneutics of suspicion, the attempt (by critics like de Man) to deconstruct the prematurely totalizing rhetoric of Romantic transcendence. The difference is that Lowes' empiricist commitment prevents him from actively *thinking through* the questions raised by this displaced encounter. De Man – to repeat the point – insists that deconstruction must always make use of 'epistemologically rigorous methods' in order to expose the limitations of those methods. Otherwise it becomes a mere interpretative game, condemned to rehearse old errors under cover of a new-found rhetoric of crisis.

Lowes is in no danger of succumbing to this, the theoreticist trap of an empty circularity engrossed by its own ruling concepts. His is the opposite case: that of a refusal to engage theoretical issues which have come to dominate the discourse of post-Romantic criticism. By willing away the idealist problematic, Lowes leaves his text always open to a 'return of the repressed' in the various uncanny forms and guises of displaced figuration. 'I am speaking in parables, I know, for there seems to be no other way; but the thing itself, however phrased, is, I believe, in its essentials, true.'[27] The difference between 'parable' and 'allegory' is perhaps a fine point of scholastic disputation. But it is fair to venture that a 'parable' claims some privileged access to revealed or intuitive truth, while 'allegory' can only hint at such meaning through a narrative sequence of *arbitrary* signposts which admit the unavailability of any transcendent, self-justifying vision. What the rhetoric of the above passage tries to achieve is a validating shift from narrative devices to a sense of mystic consummation backed up by its distinctly religious overtones. There is still the metaphysical haze of suggestion, carried by Lowes' idealizing language even where it controverts the substance of his method. From 'parable' to 'allegory' is a movement of demystification which critics like de Man are incessantly anxious to set in train. In reverse, it is precisely the valorizing gesture which Lowes rhetorically exploits to present his surrogate narrative inventions as metaphors of revealed poetic truth. His tactics of piecemeal reconstruction in the end require support from that suspect metaphysics which his method is at pains to deny.

The Road to Xanadu remains a classic of its kind, despite the perplexities engendered by its conflict of interpretative aims. This chapter has deliberately read against the grain, refusing to set aside those philosophic issues which Lowes wished to lock into the lumber-room of fusty metaphysics. Approached on its own terms – as a quest for lost origins, a psychic 'voyage' through the mysteries of creation – the book undeniably exerts a powerful hold. The reason, quite simply, is that Coleridge's sources provide copious metaphors of a strange, enchanted, exotic mental landscape which Lowes can then apply to describe the workings of Romantic imagination, without any need for tiresome detours through the thickets of speculative thought. Interpretation strives to collapse the distance between creative process and critical act. But this leads, as I have argued, to all manner of paradox when the text intermittently pauses to reflect on its own implications. Barbara Johnson arrives at a similar point in her interrogative reading of the boundaries between 'literature' and 'criticism'. Their difference, she concludes, lies perhaps only in the fact 'that criticism is more likely to be blind to the way in which its own critical difference from itself makes it, in the final analysis, literary'.[28] *The Road to Xanadu* provides a striking case of this uncanny transference at work within the rhetoric of post-Romantic interpretation.

The last two chapters have moved from 'philosophy' toward 'literary criticism', at least so far as that distinction holds up in the face of deconstructionist argument. In what follows I return to a more analytical domain, looking to recent linguistic philosophy for a means of confronting, as squarely as possible, the issues posed by deconstruction.

7

Deconstruction, naming and necessity: some logical options

I

This book has set out to challenge the idea that 'linguistic philosophy', in its Anglo-American guises, has no points of contact with French theoretical developments in the wake of Saussure. What links them at root is the principle, as Frege expressed it, that 'meaning determines reference'. Knowledge and perception are always already structured by those forms of linguistic predication which stake out the limits of admissible sense. Thus for Frege it is a question of showing that referents can only be identified if language and logic between them provide the salient criteria for picking out the object referred to. There is no direct or one-to-one relation between word, concept and referent. Naming must always depend upon a structure of predicative assumptions which mark out the object in question, defining its relevant or necessary features and thus providing a referential framework. Bertrand Russell argued to similar effect in his well-known 'theory of descriptions'. On his account, names were a species of compacted or summary definition, words which had to be unpacked, as it were, in order to identify the semantic markers which characterized their object.

Such is the 'linguistic turn' in modern philosophy, the outlook which Wittgenstein also expressed – though from a rather different viewpoint – when he declared that 'the limits of my language' are likewise and inherently 'the limits of my world'. Nor is it hard to see how this attitude squares with the structuralist emphasis on language as the omnipresent mediating element in all existing orders of knowledge and representation. Saussure laid the groundwork of a general semiotics which, basing itself to begin with on linguistic methodology, would then move out to encompass the diverse systems of cultural meaning and exchange. Central to his project was the insistence that language so completely structures and determines our grasp of the world that 'reality' can only be construed as a product of deep-laid linguistic conventions. The arbitrary nature of the sign – the Saussurean 'bar' between signifier and signified – was the token of precisely this capacity in language to shape our conceptions in accordance with its own structural economy. There is an obvious parallel here with the so-called 'Sapir-Whorf hypothesis', the argument from comparative linguistics that certain cultures (like Whorf's Hopi-Indian) have languages so structurally different from our own that they must be assumed to articulate a radically independent grasp of reality. There is no straightforward referential appeal which could override such evidence of linguistic diversity. Saussure, and the structuralists after him, acknowlege this primacy of the signifying process, and are thus set squarely against any attempt to naturalize the relation between signifier and signified.

In this respect at least, there is a good deal in common between the structuralist and logico-linguistic traditions. For Saussure as for Frege, 'meaning determines reference' in the sense that there exists no self-sufficient act of naming outside the criteria which language provides for deciding how – or on what specific terms – such an act achieves its designated object. Frege is in pursuit of a logical semantics or a basis for translating the ambiguities of natural language into a register of clear-cut referential implication. His examples of vague or indeterminate reference are designed to emphasize this need for a theory of meaning which aspires to the ideal of a demonstrative science. Saussure had no such objective in view. The linguistic 'science' he envisaged was a construct of linked or co-implicated terms ('langue', 'parole', 'synchronic', 'diachronic', etc.) which defined their own field and specific priorities *without* laying claim to any absolute grounding in epistemological truth. Certainly it follows from the structuralist argument that thought is necessarily constrained by certain regularities of language which semiological theory seeks to explain. To this extent, perhaps, the Saussurian 'science of signs' implies its own status as a meta-language equipped to interpret and 'scientifically' grasp all other forms of discourse. But this is quite distinct from the Fregean claim that semantics as 'first philosophy' is uniquely fitted to analyse the very terms of epistemological truth.

The point can be brought out more clearly by looking at a typical example from Frege. The instance is that of proper names (like 'Aristotle') which raise all manner of philosophic problem as soon as one asks what conditions apply to their use as uniquely referring terms. In such cases, Frege writes,

> opinions as regards their sense may diverge. As such may, e.g., be suggested: Plato's disciple and the teacher of Alexander the Great. Whoever accepts this sense will interpret the meaning of the statement 'Aristotle was born in Stagira', differently from one who interpreted the sense of 'Aristotle' as the Stagirite teacher of Alexander the Great. As long as the nominatum remains the same, these fluctuations in sense are tolerable. But they should be avoided in the system of a demonstrative science and should not appear in a perfect language.[1]

Frege's argument turns on the difficulty of assigning necessary or definitive attributes to names (like 'Aristotle') which no mere list or weighting of priorities can ever determine. This leads on to problems of a logical kind in deciding on the status of factual propositions. What may be informative about Aristotle in one context – since it adds some detail to the speaker's or listener's stock of associative attributes – will elsewhere seem quite redundant since it merely reduplicates some item in that stock.

Hence the need, in Frege's view, for a theory of logical and semantic implication which preserves the otherwise threatened distinction between analytic and synthetic judgments. That Aristotle was a Stagirite, that he taught Alexander, that he studied with Plato and authored *The Poetics* – these are all attributes which may or may not figure in the semantic construct which is Aristotle's name. Thus a Fregean analysis is called for to prevent the collapse into logical undecidability which threatens as soon as one makes any statement *about* Aristotle. The theory of descriptions comes in to explain that such acts of predication have to do with a complex of necessary and contingent attributes, and not with some uniquely determined referent, Aristotle *ipse* and everything about him.

Structuralism of course goes a different way around in its challenge to the referential function of language. Its concern is not to provide some alternative, more rigorous or 'demonstrative' means of conceptualizing language and logic. Rather, it tends to question any such project by stressing the extent to which theories or philosophies of language are themselves bound up with linguistic convention.[2] Thus Derrida, for one, sets out to deconstruct the sovereign rationality of western thought, the 'metaphysics of presence' everywhere secreted by a language ontologically blind to its own constitutive figures and metaphors.[3] Like Nietzsche before him, Derrida perceives both the necessity and the impossible nature of this task, since even the most vigilant critique of language must in the end fall victim to its own best insights. What Derrida provides – most strikingly in his texts on Plato, Nietzsche and Saussure – is a discourse which combines an extreme sceptical rigour with a wayward, unsettling figurative play designed to exploit the duplicity of language and show up its aberrant (or self-deconstructing) moments.

In so doing, he can claim a scrupulous fidelity to the letter (if not the spirit) of texts which uncannily work to undo their own 'logocentric' assumptions. Structuralism figures for Derrida as the last and most acutely contradictory form of this play between blindness and insight, metaphysics and the textual 'unconscious' wherein its ruses are pre-empted and dismantled. The very notion of 'structure', he argues, is a metaphor which passes itself off as a concept, striving to contain and articulate the endless disseminating energies of language. Structuralism lives on what Derrida describes as 'the difference between its promise and its practice'. Deconstruction on the contrary sets out to demonstrate 'the principled, essential, and structural impossibility of closing a structural phenomenology'.[4]

This radical critique of meaning and method is clearly worlds apart from the Fregean demand for epistemological clarity. All the same it can be argued that Derrida has simply pushed to an extreme – perverse though some might think it – the principle embodied in Frege's dictum that 'meaning determines reference'. That scepticism has a logic of its own, not to be halted by compromise measures, is a lesson to be drawn from more than one episode of philosophic history. Nietzsche's critique of Kant is a pointedly relevant example. Kant thought to rescue philosophy from the abysmal snares of sceptical doubt by insisting that its proper concern was not to prove that the mind could 'know' reality – could achieve, that is, a direct and unmediated knowledge – but to show how experience was always and inevitably *structured* by the innate constitution of human intelligence. The categories of understanding and judgment could thus stand proof against sceptical attack by claiming to be the sole, constitutive ground of intelligible order. The sceptic might deny their validity, but only at the cost of condemning his own arguments to solipsism or manifest absurdity. It remained for Nietzsche to call what he saw as the Kantian bluff. Why should thought submit to the claims of a 'rational' philosophy whose *a priori* structure might simply reflect a present inability to think beyond its own, self-imposed limits? Why should the categories of Kantian philosophy hold themselves immune from the sceptical critique which applied to everything outside their elective domain? Was Kant not repeating the age-old logocentric gesture, inaugurated by Socrates in his dealing with the sophists and other such 'irrational' thinkers? This, according to Nietzsche, was the ploy by which reason had always worked to repress or marginalize everything which threatened its sovereign grasp.

Nietzsche's critique of Kant is precisely analogous to Derrida's deconstruction of the concepts and metaphors involved in structuralist discourse. In each case there is a challenge to the philosophic gesture which strives to hold scepticism at bay by setting up new limits and (within them) absolute powers for the sovereignty of reason. Such philosophies must always be strategically blind to the fact that they rest upon a willed regime of choices and exclusions, a 'structured genealogy' of concepts which maintains the appearance of distinterested reason. In Derrida and Nietzsche, deconstruction takes the form of locating these loaded oppositions, showing how they work to determine every detail of philosophic argument and thus – implicitly – how concepts are undone by the effects of that structural repression which holds them in place. Thus structuralism, in its scientistic guise, keeps up the appearances of method only by clinging to the notion of 'structure', itself a spatial *metaphor* disguised as an operative *concept*. Niezsche perceived this process at work in each successive stage of philosophical 'enlightenment'. From Socrates to Kant, the claims of right reason had advanced under cover of a will-to-power blind to its own constitutive metaphors but quick to denounce all signs of 'irrational' or figurative thought in its opponents. Derrida's texts take up this critique with the additional refinement or leverage supplied by a post-Saussurean linguistic topology. Where Nietzsche saw a generalized rhetorical drift – from originating metaphor to sublimating concept – Derrida spells out the textual operations which mark this strategy in Plato, Rousseau, Saussure, or indeed Nietzsche himself.

Deconstruction is philosophy of language at its most self-critical and Nietzschean stage. Derrida would claim to have interpreted structuralism, not so much against itself as in accordance with the deconstructive logic which works from within both to generate its most powerful insights and to criticize, implicitly, its blind-spots of 'logocentric' closure. Thus his essay on Saussure (in *Of Grammatology*) raises the problematic of 'writing' as opposed to 'speech', most crucial of the structured oppositions which Derrida sees as determining the entire genealogy of western metaphysics:

> It is when he is not expressly dealing with writing, when he feels he has closed the parentheses on that subject, that Saussure opens the field of a general grammatology ... then one realizes that what was chased off limits, the wandering outcast of linguistics, has indeed never ceased to haunt language as its primary and most intimate possibility.[5]

The deconstructive leverage exerted by the topos of 'writing' comes of its challenge to the notion of speech as self-presence, a notion which – as Derrida shows – runs deep and far back in the history of western philosophy. In various figurative forms its workings are denounced and visibly repressed, only to resurface in Derrida's readings as a challenge to the metaphysics of Plato, the Rousseauist philosophy of nature and origins, the phenomenological reasonings of Husserl and – as here – the remnant logocentrism of Saussure. Writing is the 'wandering outcast' of language in its power to disrupt all self-possessed philosophies of meaning and knowledge.

From the deconstructionist standpoint, Derrida's texts represent not only the determinate outcome of structuralist thought, but also the most rigorous following-through of the 'linguistic turn' in modern philosophy generally. As Nietzsche stood to the mainstream tradition of nineteenth-century epistemology, so Derrida stands to its latter-day counterpart, wherein the problems of knowledge and perception have been largely recast in linguistic terms. Richard Rorty has described the situation as follows, with Russell and Frege specifically in mind:

> 'Analytic' philosophy is one more variant of Kantian philosophy, a variant marked principally by thinking of representation as linguistic rather than mental, and of philosophy of language rather than 'transcendental critique', or psychology, as the discipline which exhibits the 'foundations of knowledge'.[6]

The linguistic turn is simply another variant of the quest for first principles and cognitive assurance which sets philosophy up as the master-discipline of knowledge.

Rorty sees this whole tradition as captive to its own ruling metaphors, notably that which he takes for the title of his book, *Philosophy and the Mirror of Nature*. From Plato to Descartes, Kant and beyond, philosophers have grounded their arguments in the idea of Mind as a source of more or less accurate, detailed or conceptually satisfying representations. Kant's 'revolution', though it shifted the emphasis from a passive to an active version of this process, still sought its truths in accordance with the same underlying specular metaphor. Epistemology took up the task of 'inspecting, repairing, and polishing the mirror', all with the aim of 'getting more accurate representations'.[7] And linguistic philosophy in recent times has been largely devoted, Rorty maintains, to preserving this ambition through a different set of analytic techniques.

It is against this background that the claims of deconstruction come to bear on the wider practice of linguistic philosophy. That 'meaning determines reference' is a large and potentially unlimited concession to what Derrida would call the 'disseminating' power of language. To hold such a principle within the bounds of epistemological reason, one needs a logical semantics which can clearly distinguish between necessary (analytic) structures of meaning and senses which cannot or need not be thus construed. And it is precisely this confident Kantian distinction which – as Rorty argues – has come under increasing strain in recent philosophy. Thinkers like Quine, starting out from a broadly pragmatist position, have discovered no grounds for preserving the notion of *a priori* logical necessity. Quine describes the total field of knowledge at any given time as 'a man-made fabric which impinges on experience only along the edges'. Any conflicts with experience eventually cause 're-adjustments in the interior of the field'. Supposedly *a priori* truths are themselves so linked to the total structure of knowledge that they may at any time be subject to revision, the field as a whole being 'undetermined by its boundary conditions'.[8] This is effectively to collapse the distinction between synthetic and analytic judgments.

It is perhaps time to summarize my main points of argument so far. Analytic philosophy of language is committed to pre-serving certain crucial relations between meaning and logical necessity. At the same time it suspends or elects to disregard the directly *referential* function of language, seeking its epistemologi-cal ground in determinate structures of logico-semantic implica-tion. To this extent it shares the structuralist view that meanings are produced by the articulated network of elements and con-trasts which make up language as a whole (Saussure's *la langue*). Where it differs, on Frege's or Russell's account, is in requiring that logic should distinguish between 'contingent' and 'neces-sary' attributes of sense, such that a word's meaning – thus analysed – is capable of meeting the requirement of unambi-guous sense. Meaning therefore 'precedes reference' only to the point, and in the interest, of securing the latter from acute semantic instability. But this programme, as I have argued, is rendered problematic as soon as one asks how limits can be set to those 'fluctuations of sense' which Frege (in his passage on 'Aristotle') sought to keep within tolerable bounds. Nietzsche and Derrida, Quine and Rorty each raise doubts as to the prospects of maintaining this regime of logical necessity. To suspend the referential function of language is to open pros-pects of semantic slippage or undecidability which Derrida has exploited to maximum effect. His critique of structuralism in its scientistic moment might well extend to the domain of analytic philosophy of language.

II

To reverse Frege's dictum and assert the priority of reference over meaning would, of course, create a very marked shift of philosophical assumptions. One such line of argument is advanced by Saul Kripke in his lectures published under the title *Naming and Necessity*.[9] Kripke writes a disarmingly colloquial prose but sets out nevertheless to question and replace most of the ruling conventions in current analytic philosophy. His arguments should also be of interest to those critical theorists uneasy with the way in which deconstruction seems to sever all links between language and reality. In fact that severance is always already produced by theories of knowledge or meaning which privilege *representation* in whatever epistemological guise. Kripke's claims can therefore be seen as a challenge to that entire tradition of thought which constitutes, in Rorty's view, the prevailing but deeply problematic post-Kantian consensus. They amount to a case for totally revising the accepted picture of language, truth and logic.

Kripke's argument can be briefly summarized as follows. Naming, he contends, is a matter of 'rigid designation', of using such terms as can properly be used to pick out the referent in question. The paradigm case is that of 'fixing a reference', rather than (as Frege or Russell would argue) applying a set of descriptive attributes which enable one to identify the object referred to. The latter theory can be shown to run into all kinds of logical perplexity. Thus for instance – to return to Frege's example – one might include among the necessary truths about Aristotle the fact that he was 'the greatest man who studied with Plato', or 'the last great philosopher of antiquity'. According to the Russell-Frege analysis, these facts would (either or both) make up the effective *definition* of the name 'Aristotle'. But, as Kripke points out, this leads to insuperable problems if one postulates some other 'possible world' or set of alternative *données*. If Aristotle turned out *not* in fact to have studied with Plato – or if some other candidate were presented as 'the last great philosopher of antiquity' – then the logic of identity would break down entirely. One would have to conclude, in effect, that 'Aristotle' was not Aristotle. In fact it would have to be the other man who bore that name. Kripke's idea of 'rigid designation' claims to resolve this and similar quandaries. 'If we merely use the description to *fix the referent* then that man will be the referent of "Aristotle" in all possible worlds' (Kripke, p.13).

Kripke offers many such examples, not all of them involving proper names. Some have to do with natural phenomena (like 'light' and 'sound') which might seem grist to the descriptivist mill since the very possibility of naming them as such might be held to depend on our knowing how to recognize their attributes or effects. But, Kripke asks, would we therefore have to say that, if everyone were blind, light would no longer exist? Clearly not, he replies; rather we would say that 'light – the thing we have identified as that which in fact enables us to see – existed but did not manage to help us see due to some defect in us' (Kripke, p.130). One might go on to imagine yet further 'possible worlds' of even more extravagant remoteness. What if certain creatures, otherwise 'human' in every respect, were insensitive to light (photons) but responded to sound-waves in exactly the same way that we respond to light? In this case, Kripke argues, we should *not* be reduced – as the descriptivist would have it – to using 'light' as a name synomymous with 'whatever gives us the visual impression – whatever helps us to see'. Quite simply, 'there might have been light and it not helped us to see; and even something else might have helped us to see'(Kripke, p.131). The only way out of this awkward situation is to give up the descriptivist quest for a grounding theory of necessary attributes. For Kripke, 'the way we identified light *fixed a reference*'.

What Kripke's arguments come down to is a programme for re-writing philosophical semantics on a post-Kantian and, by implication, a neo-Aristotelian basis. As Rorty describes it, the Kripkean injunction is to say 'we'll call *that* X', rather than saying 'we'll call something X if it meets the following criteria...'.[10] To take another example, it might be held that 'gold' was necessarily identified in part as being yellow in colour. What would be the consequence, Kripke asks, if it emerged that in fact this apparent yellowness was an optical illusion created by certain local atmospheric conditions? Would we have to say that gold no longer existed, since nothing now satisfied the relevant definitional criteria? No, says Kripke, for the necessary reason that 'we as part of a community of speakers have a certain connection between ourselves and a certain kind of thing' (in this case gold) (Kripke, p.118). Though of course it may happen that descriptive criteria change in the light of new knowledge, this does not entail the occasional overnight abandonment of names and their notional referents. What in fact we have discovered are certain properties pertaining to gold and henceforth standing in for others which no longer apply. 'These properties, then, being characteristic of gold and not true of iron pyrites, show that the fool's gold is not in fact gold' (Kripke, p.119).

Kripke's examples are from one point of view a means of preserving commonsense usage against the kinds of specialized redescription evolved by modern science. Thus 'light' may be defined as a stream of photons, or – complementarily – a form of electromagnetic radiation. But these descriptions, he argues, cannot displace the 'original' or designative sense, namely that which identifies 'light' by 'the characteristic internal visual impressions it can produce in us, that make us able to see' (Kripke, p.129). The technical adjustments of scientific language cannot, on this account, radically change the primary reference which constitutes their field of application. There has to subsist a certain referential grounding without which no such refinement of theory could retain its grasp on the phenomena concerned.'We fix what light is by the fact that it is whatever, out in the world, affects our eyes in a certain way' (Kripke, p.130).

This argument clearly has large consequences for epistemological theory as conceived in logico-semantic terms. It also implies a fairly drastic critique of the structuralist (or post-structuralist) contention that meaning is a product of the signifying patterns and contrasts which determine the semantic economy of language (*la langue*). Kripke's proposal can be read, in this context, as arguing a full-scale reversal of Saussure's founding precept: that the signified is always already constructed by the system of interrelated signifiers which bring it into play. This amounts to a denial of the 'arbitrary' nature of the sign, and a move to re-establish the referential function denied to language in all varieties of post-Saussurean discourse. It asserts the case for determinate reference as a necessary presupposition of any attempt to make sense of language on logically coherent terms.

Kripke's arguments bring up a wide range of philosophic issues in support of his central claim. For one thing, they entail a notion of necessity, linked to that of naming or rigid designation, which largely revises conventional ideas about truth-conditional semantics. Kripke, like Rorty, finds fault with most accepted formulations of the distinction between analytic and synthetic judgments. He rejects, that is to say, the Kantian structure of assumptions and its various latter-day successors in the logico-semantic line. If the theory of descriptions rests (as we have seen) on precisely such a basis of epistemological assumption, then so much the worse for that theory. There are so-called 'analytic' truths (the example 'gold is yellow' is actually taken from Kant) which might conceivably turn out to be false in some other possible world. Likewise there are cases where certainty (an 'epistemological notion') need not coexist with any kind of absolute or *a priori* truth:

> Something can be known, or at least rationally believed, *a priori*, without being quite certain, You've read a proof in the math book; and, though you think it's correct, maybe you've made a mistake. You often do make mistakes of this kind. You've made a computation, perhaps with an error.[11]

What Kripke is showing in these examples is the breakdown of epistemological theory and the need for introducing a different notion of 'necessity', one which decisively rejects the principle that 'meaning determines reference'.

Kripke is not claiming – indeed he is at pains to deny – that his is a better 'theory' for coping with the problems encountered by current analytical philosophy. Rather, he is trying to shift the ground so completely that those problems either disappear or come to seem specialized puzzles on the margins of attainable knowledge. His argument throughout is that this way of seeing things corresponds to the normal or intuitive mode of naming which obtains in the great majority of practical situations. Kripke accepts that some philosophers (i.e. the descriptivists) 'think that something's having intuitive content is very inconclusive evidence in favor of it'. He asks, on the contrary, 'what more conclusive evidence one can have about anything, ultimately speaking?' (Kripke, p.42). Those who deny the link between naming and necessity have allowed a sophisticated philosophic theory to reverse the very nature and conditions of intuitive judgment. Yet, as he readily admits, the descriptivist case does possess (in certain problematic areas) a 'marvelous internal coherence' which explains its lasting appeal. What Kripke is putting forward is a whole set of reasons for *preferring* his rival account, and for not continuing to treat it as naïve, outworn or philosophically bankrupt. He is claiming, in short, 'that the natural intuition that the names of ordinary language are rigid designators can in fact be upheld' (Kripke, p.5).

III

I have suggested already that close parallels exist between the assumptions of analytic philosophy and the view of language more or less taken for granted in post-structuralist theory. It remains to make out a case for testing, and perhaps revising, that view in the light of Kripke's powerful critique. Structuralism starts out from the premise that language is so organized as to constitute our only means of access to a shared world of objects and experience. The 'arbitrary' nature of the sign – the lack of any natural bond between signifier and signified – necessitates the theory that reference is always dependent on meaning, and meaning itself bound up with a structured economy of signifying relationships and differences. This contention is often supported by empirical observations, like the fact that different linguistic cultures have strikingly different ways of dividing up the spectrum of colours.[12] It is held to lead on to the generalized idea that 'reality' is always already constructed by the 'discourse', or ensemble of signifying practices, used to describe or explain it.

　　This position is much akin to that of the philosopher Quine, who (as we have seen) brings a radically pragmatist argument to bear on the distinction between analytic and synthetic judgments. For Quine this entails the further consequence that translation between languages is always impossible, since there is no appeal to the kind of clear-cut logico-semantic analysis which would offer firm definitional criteria. Quine's thesis finds a parallel in the 'structural genealogy' of knowledge argued by Michel Foucault. Cultural epochs are defined in terms of the prevalent 'discourse', or paradigm of representations, which sets an effective limit to the forms of available knowledge. This applies not only to the so-called 'sciences of man' but also to the natural sciences which organize their data in accordance with certain deep-lying but ultimately relative and changeable paradigms of order. The historical sequence of such major mutations of discourse is Foucault's theme in his book *The Order of Things*.[13] Its theoretical basis can best be described as a bringing-together of Saussure's central thesis – the primacy of signifying practice – with a Nietzschean stress on the arbitrary will-to-power implicit in all claims to knowledge.

Deconstruction represents a further stage in this resolute critique of the assumptions which prop up our normal idea of the relation between language and reality. To deconstruct a text, in Derridean terms, is to bring out a radical disjunction between logic and rhetoric, intention and sense, what language explicitly *says* and what its figural workings constrain it to *mean*. These techniques are not – as many detractors have claimed – a species of sophisticated verbal sport with anomalies entirely engendered by their own perverse will to problematize language. Deconstruction is the rigorous consequence, not only of structuralist thinking but of any linguistic philosophy basing its methods on the principle that 'meaning determines [or precedes] reference'. Derrida's procedures are not the less compelling for the fact that they work to question or confound all normative concepts of logic and meaning. His arguments are the outcome of a Nietzschean principled scepticism, allied to the means of linguistic analysis provided by Saussure.

Responses to Derrida – and to post-structuralist theory in general – tend to take a line of flatly commonsense assertion. What remains of language if its hold on reality is always delusive, a product of meanings which self-deconstruct in the very process of description or argument? Is it not a simple case (asks Gerald Graff) of intellectuals retreating from the harsh conflicts of social experience into a realm of unlimited 'textuality' where problems are always safely contained because dreamed up to order in the first place?[14] And if deconstruction leaves us bereft of any grasp on material reality, what remains of the other, interior life of subjective meaning and commitment? John Searle, as we have seen, takes Derrida to task for his 'wilful' misreading of Austin, his assertion that speech-acts are a matter of conventionalized (or 'iterable') formulae, devoid of authentic guarantee.[15] Derrida responds with a text of riddling semantic virtuosity designed to expropriate Austin – and language in general – from the vested proprietory claims of an interpreter like Searle.[16] Mischievously quoting whole chunks of Searle's essay in a radically alien context, Derrida makes his point yet again: that language is always caught up in a play of multiple signifying games which make it impossible to fix either its reference or the subjective intent behind it. Speech-acts are examples of a 'generalized iterability' which marks all forms of intelligible utterance, Austin's and Searle's included.

Deconstruction is proof against any line of attack which situates itself on commonsense ground, or which flatly refuses to countenance the problems raised by epistemological scepticism. On their own terms its strategies possess the same kind of cogent demonstrative power, or 'marvelous internal coherence', that Kripke has to concede to the descriptivist case. Language itself, as de Man argues, 'dissociates the cognition from the act', opening a gap between the surface or purported meaning and the structures of rhetorical implication which work to undo it. The illusion of reference is achieved by constantly repressing or effacing this constitutive duplicity in language. Straightforward understanding requires that we ignore what de Man describes as the disjunction between rhetoric and grammar, or 'the semantic function and the formal structure of language'.[17] But this commonsense attitude involves a degree of interpretative blindness (conscious or unconscious) that de Man often treats as tantamount to sheer bad faith. Language and reading succeed in maintaining the referential illusion 'only at the cost of a subterfuge to which it finds itself necessarily condemned'.[18]

The importance of Kripke's arguments in this context is that they offer an alternative account of meaning and reference which strongly resists any such charge of epistemological innocence. They are strong enough, that is, to provide an analytic framework (built on the link between naming and necessity) which holds up to sceptical attack. This is not to say that they render deconstruction irrelevant or 'logically' untenable. Rorty states the case as follows with reference to Kripke *versus* the Frege-Russell tradition:

> One can play it either way, and develop a system from either starting-point with equal completeness and elegance. In either case, the budget of paradoxes will be about equally long, though much will depend upon what one has been brought up to find paradoxical.[19]

To decide, in this way, that the issue is finally undecidable is not to reduce it to mere triviality. The force of Kripke's arguments is sufficient, Rorty says, to have 'pointed semantics in a new direction', and thus made it possible to reformulate problems which were hidden or ruled out of court on the alternative view.

Of course the deconstructor can come back at this point and argue that such 'rigorous undecidability' is precisely the upshot of her readings. Deconstruction thrives on the radical incommensurability of rhetoric and logic, meaning and structure, 'naïve' and critical interpretation. It could find few better examples than what Rorty calls the 'stand-off' between Russell-Fregean and Kripkean semantics, each possessed of its own very cogent rationale. Again, deconstruction would have the last word *on its own chosen terms of debate*. Yet it still remains the case that such undecidability logically requires an adversary discourse of sufficient cogency and strength to produce the looked-for deconstructionist *aporia*. Derrida and de Man would be tilting at metaphysical windmills if the 'naïve' readings they measure themselves against were really as naïve as all that. At present the climate of polemical exchange is such that both sides are forced into deadlocked and intransigent postures. Opponents fall back on a rhetoric of commonsense empirical bluff, while the deconstructors – or some of them – exercise their wits on a phantom array of metaphysical delusions. What Kripke provides – to repeat – is one powerful redefinition of what it takes to be consequent and rigorous in thinking about language. An engagement with Kripkean semantics on the deconstructors' part would not so much disqualify as properly and reciprocally *deconstruct* their own more facile assumptions.

'The signifier, though to all appearances freely chosen with respect to the idea that it represents, is fixed, not free, with respect to the linguistic community that uses it.'[20] Saussure makes several such statements in the *Course in General Linguistics*, intended to qualify his doctrine of the arbitrary nature of the sign. Without this provision it is impossible to pass from an abstract conceptualization of language – *la langue* – to a grasp of its communicative workings and social nature. In effect Saussure has to make room for the basic Kripkean contention: that reference is always to some degree 'fixed' in relation to the communal norms which govern linguistic exchange. Kripke indeed offers statements of his position which closely parallel Saussure's formulation. He speaks of 'the predominantly social character' of reference, and the fact that 'we use names to communicate with speakers in a common language' (Kripke, p.163).

The deconstructionist could clearly argue that this leaves an element of crucial undecidability at the heart of Kripkean semantics. What becomes of this so-called 'rigid designation' – the link between naming and necessity – if speakers, for instance, misapply names or transfer them to different (maybe fictitious) entities? Kripke actually anticipates this line of objection. He offers the example of 'Madagascar', originally the native designation for a part of Africa, but subsequently misinterpreted by Marco Polo as the name of an island. In such cases, he argues, the substitute ('mistaken') reference has become so common that it must override the obscured historical origin. 'Real reference can shift to another real reference, fictional reference can shift to real, and real to fictional' (Kripke, p.163). The deconstructionist would no doubt seize on such a passage as opening the way to all manner of referential slippage and undecidability, as Derrida does in his determined assaults on the arbitrary protocols of meaning and truth. Kripke would respond by pointing to the fact that a marginal case like 'Madagascar' already presupposes a certain background of conflicting but still operative referential claims. To concede its ambiguity is already to possess a well-defined idea of what reference properly entails.

Kripke can therefore defend his position here with the same line of argument as he brings against the Fregean descriptivists. Their particular kinds of problem would only occur to those speakers who have mastered a complex theory of reference, and it would be this theory, of course, and not the speaker's knowledge of a description, which gave the true picture of how the reference was determined.[21]

The case is much the same with the post-structuralist challenge to 'naïve' or referential readings of texts. Without some implicitly well-defined notion of what reference entails, a critic like de Man would be *logically* unable to deconstruct its claims. The paradoxical upshot is that linguistic scepticism can only elaborate its case by preserving intact, within its own conceptual structure, the very notions it seeks to discredit.

Such might be outline of a Kripkean riposte to the claims of deconstruction. Of course the whole argument could be turned round yet again if the deconstructor were to fasten, for instance, on the metaphors of origin which Kripke resorts to in his account of language. He often appears to imply the existence of an originating act or 'baptism' of naming which can then serve as a *terminus a quo* for the chain of communal transmission which preserves the fixity of reference. Kripke concedes at one point that 'there need not always be an identifiable initial baptism' (Kripke, p.162), but elsewhere his arguments distinctly entertain the idea. Thus naming is construed as most often entailing the necessity that 'a speaker intends to use a name in the same way as it was transmitted to him' (Kripke, p.163). It is hard to sustain this theory *without* some generalized idea of an 'initial baptism'. And Derrida (in *Of Grammatology*) has textual strategies in plenty for showing up the self-deconstructing and illusory character of all such myths of origin.

It remains, as I have argued, important to preserve a philosophically cogent alternative to linguistic scepticism. Kripke provides just such a basis for controverting post-structuralist theory at its own sophisticated level. That 'the game can be played both ways', in Rorty's words, is a vital recognition given the current distracting flurry of confused polemical exchange. Marxist and historical criticism especially stand to gain by discovering some way beyond the extreme theoretical contortions induced by their struggle to counter this challenge. When Hayden White (in his book *Metahistory*) examines the narrative

and tropological devices involved in historical texts, his
methods are seen as an out-and-out denial of history itself and
the historian's claim to knowledge.[22] Among the Marxists this
hostility is sharpened by their lately having shared certain
similar post-structuralist techniques of demystification. Terry
Eagleton has moved from an elaborately argued critique of
ideology and representation[23] to a blistering attack on deconstructionist theory as a species of textual fixation designed to
keep history and politics at bay. Deconstruction is cast as

> a sort of patient, probing reformism of the text, which is
> not, so to speak, to be confronted over the barricades but
> cunningly waylaid in the corridors and suavely chivvied into
> revealing its ideological hand.[24]

The hostility often comes of a drastically dualist conviction, that
language must *either* engage directly with historical realities *or*
deconstruct itself in a timeless aporia of pure textuality.

Can such fundamental quarrels really be affected by a shift of
semantic presupposition? Rorty suggests an affirmative answer
when he points out that Marxist (and neo-Thomist) thinkers
were among the few to resist the ascendance of epistemological
theory in its modern logico-semantic form.[25] Their basically
Aristotelian standpoint anticipated Kripke's conception of language, though lacking its particular forms of elaborated argument. Kripkean semantics therefore has a distinct and more
than technical bearing on the issues raised by Eagleton. It
affords a theory of referential meaning not immune to deconstruction but capable of meeting its challenge on equal and
opposite terms. As such it might bring about a very welcome
sharpening of focus in current theoretical debate.

Methodological postscript: deconstruction versus interpretation?

'Against interpretation' has become something of watchword among recent literary theorists. Susan Sontag coined the phrase in the title of a much-quoted essay[1] forecasting the demise of interpretative criticism and calling for something more adventurous, pleasurable, polyperverse; an 'erotics of the text' such as Roland Barthes was later to suggest.[2] Since then the call has come from different quarters and with various divergent ends in view. Structuralism looked for a way beyond the vagaries of mere interpretation by proposing a 'science' of applied poetics, possessed of a coherent methodology and raising its sights above the individual text to the defining characteristics of literary discourse at large. Tzvetan Todorov went so far as to argue that this had always been the object of critics, from Aristotle down, who required something more of their discipline than a loose assemblage of *ad hoc* isolated insights.[3] For Todorov, the history of criticism could be seen as a series of unfortunate lapses from Aristotelian rigour into mere impressionistic or interpretative flair. This decline was arrested only by those occasional formalist 'revivals' of which the present age had witnessed its share. Todorov writes as a convinced neo-formalist to whom structuralism represents a welcome source of sharpened linguistic and theoretical perceptions.

As this scientistic dream receded, so erstwhile 'structuralists' like Barthes began to question the very concept of critical *method*, especially as applied to the plural and protean texts which most engaged their interest. Derrida gave a lead to this questioning in his rigorously argued deconstruction of everything that passed for conceptual clarity in western philosophical tradition. Rhetoric and logic were seen to be at odds, with rhetoric always, in the last (textual) analysis, working to complicate the purposes of logical thought. The concept of 'structure' was one of those which Derrida deconstructed in order to demonstrate their covert reliance on suppressed metaphorical energies and tensions.[4] It could only take hold, he argued, by a species of conceptual will-to-power, a ploy which aspired to the status of theory but which rested, nevertheless, on metaphors and figural displacements beyond its imaginary sovereign control.

Derrida's influence was clearly at work in this shift from 'structuralist' to 'post-structuralist' modes of textual engagement. A work like Barthes' *S/Z* (1970) reflected this shift in its utopian desire to liberate the plural energies of writing from the protocols of formal analysis.[5] Where Barthes had once looked for a 'grammar' of narrative functions[6] – a full-scale applied poetics in Todorov's sense – he now set about to deconstruct that scientistic myth by dispersing the elements of Balzac's text, subjecting it to a reading at once obsessively minute and wildly exorbitant. The idea of 'structure' gave way to that of 'structuration', an activity which recognized no proper or constitutive limits to the production of meaning in and around the multiple codes of the text. *S/Z* made play with the clanking machinery of structuralist analysis, but only in order to expose it to the polymorphous pleasures of a textual economy beyond its power to comprehend.

Yet this excess of meaning over method is not to be construed as a return to 'interpretation' in anything like the traditional sense of the word. For all its appearance of dazzling inventiveness – some would say perverse ingenuity – *S/Z* is not concerned to present merely a novel or striking interpretative slant on Balzac's text. *Sarrasine* may provide a peculiarly apt example of how narratives – even 'classic realist' narratives – can be seen to buckle and self-deconstruct under the strain of their own textual production. But implicit throughout Barthes's reading is the claim that some such process is at work in any narrative sufficiently extended or complex to justify the analyst's attention. At this stage Barthes has decisively broken with the ethos of methodological rigour which marked his earlier excursions into narrative theory. What takes its place is a different but no less rigorous concern to essay the limits of structural analysis and – correlatively – the problems and paradoxes of narrative representation.

Jonathan Culler is prominent among those who have called for an end to the workaday business of 'interpreting' texts. In his *Structuralist Poetics* (1975) Culler argued, like Todorov, that criticism had much better concern itself with the deep-lying systems and structures of convention which make up the 'grammar' of competent literary response.[7] This would place it, if not on a 'scientific' footing, at least on a basis of rational, concerted enquiry very different from the mere piling-up of variant individual readings. Culler's closing chapter takes brief account of Derridean deconstruction and other, more politicized forms of post-structuralist activity. That they figure, at this stage, as marginal developments is a consequence of Culler's perceiving very clearly that deconstruction threatens to undermine the very grounds and rationale of his structuralist project.

In *The Pursuit of Signs* (1981), Culler has come round to a different way of thinking, one which sees deconstruction as the upshot and rigorous following-through of structuralist thought.[8] His argument is still 'against interpretation' and committed to the quest for a critical enterprise beyond the vagaries of impressionistic insight. To this end he urges that criticism should see itself as part of a larger semiological programme devoted to the systematic study of signs, discourse and communicative contexts in general. However – so his argument runs – semiotics has to recognize certain crucial problems within its own methodology which call for deconstructionist analysis. The promise of a full-scale totalizing *method* is undone by the inbuilt tendency of signifying systems to create paradoxical effects and conflicts of meaning which admit of no ultimate resolution. Culler's essays in *The Pursuit of Signs* are concerned to bring out the workings of this strange double logic which seems to inhabit both 'literary' texts and the critical-interpretative effort to master their meaning. Deconstruction thus becomes a more canny and rigorous successor to the enterprise broached in *Structuralist Poetics*. It claims, that is to say, a degree of methodological refinement consisting precisely in its power to deconstruct the premature 'methods' of a first-order semiotics.

Deconstruction can therefore be seen as continuing the structuralist offensive 'against interpretation', or at least against
those habits of thought which characterize literary studies in
their currently predominant guise. Some would argue, indeed,
that 'American deconstruction' is unworthy of the name precisely on the grounds of its tendency to lapse into mere interpretative novelty. Rodolphe Gasché has published a number of
essays which take the 'literary' deconstructors to task for their
failure to observe this self-denying ordinance.[9] Gasché writes of
a 'double error' that has infected much of what currently passes
for deconstructionist criticism. 'Defining it as a method' and
'aiming it at the self-reflexivity of texts' are the two main sources
of confusion. Such misunderstanding was sure to come about,
Gasché writes,

> once deconstruction was imported into literary criticism, into
> an institution where a thinking enterprise becomes im-
> mediately transformed into a mechanical device by the pres-
> sures of the profession to apply and to perform.[10]

The implicit targets of his criticism are those, like J. Hillis Miller,
who came to deconstruction via a generalized concern with the
self-reflexive properties and figural dimensions of literary language. For such critics deconstruction arrived very much on
time, as a handy source of 'philosophical' grounding for what
remained, all the same, a species of thematic or interpretative
thought.

Gasché writes as a purist deconstructor who seeks to recall the
discipline to its proper domain of rigour and textual specificity.
He rejects what he views as a facile misuse of deconstructionist
'techniques' by critics whose thinking is largely fixated on such
post-Romantic themes as the subject/object dichotomy, the
self-reflexive nature of language and the regress of meaning
which these open up. To dwell on such topics as literary *themes*
is to invite the nowadays familiar charge that deconstruction
merely seizes upon texts in pursuit of its own routine preoccupations. Thus an anti-deconstructionist like Gerald Graff[11] can
argue that the current theorists are simply re-enacting the same
old mystified conceptual dilemmas that bedevilled the Romantic
poet-philosophers. Graff quotes a sentence of Paul de Man
which refers to the 'wound of a fracture that lies hidden in all

texts'. If this is the case, he protests, then 'the deconstructor's uncovering of the wound in any particular text becomes tautological and trivial'.[12] Gasché concedes that this charge might apply to those current *deformations professionelles* which pervert deconstruction to literary-critical ends. Indeed, he argues, such practices are deeply complicit with Graff's strategic misunderstanding of the issues at stake. They both derive from a common error: that of assimilating deconstruction to a vague thematics of textual ambivalence and 'self-reflexivity'. To this extent Graff appears justified when he writes of the 'rigged-in-advance' aspect of deconstruction, its tendency – in certain hands – to interpret every text in the light of its own pre-emptive thematic concerns. But his criticisms lack all force – according to Gasché – when measured against the rigour of such *echt*-deconstructors as Derrida and de Man.

Gasché's argument deserves close attention, not least because it might be seen as challenging my own appropriation of Derridean 'themes' in the preceding chapters. The context, again, is his reading of the issue between Graff and de Man, an issue which in turn throws up the question of what should properly *count* as deconstructionist criticism. Gasché states the case as follows:

> De Man's assertion that 'a wound of a fracture lies hidden in all texts' does not refer to a determination of the text in themes of self-reflexivity, that is, a historical and thematic determination, but it aims at textuality as such. To call the textual instance a wound of a fracture is undoubtedly a romantic image, but it is also an image for the performative rhetorics that always interrupt and render possible the cognitive rhetorics that in turn constitute the self-reflexive strata of texts.... De Man is not concerned with discovering the 'wound of a fracture' in all texts: rather, he is engaged in an active exploration of the wound in question to determine the nature and structure of a text in general.[13]

This passage goes as far as possible toward excluding (*de jure*) all forms of 'thematic' interest from the zone of deconstructionist analysis. It could even be taken to argue that literary critics have no proper business with deconstruction, unless (that is) they forsake their interpretative calling and apply themselves rather to that branch of philosophical rhetoric concerned with 'texts in general'. Such, after all, is the proper domain of Derridean grammatology.

One might all the same be inclined to question the extreme rigorist assumptions of Gasché's argument. Are his claims indeed borne out by the exemplary practice (as he sees it) of Derridean deconstruction? Is it a perverse misreading of Derrida's *Of Grammatology* which notes the deconstructive leverage exerted by such cardinal motives as *writing, supplement, trace* and their various co-implicated terms? It is no doubt the case, as Gasché contends, that these are caught up within a complex economy of textual functions, such that their sense is irreducible to any self-sufficient concept or 'theme'. They possess, that is to say, a generalized pertinence that presumably extends beyond the text in question to all varieties of (written or spoken) discourse. Yet the fact remains that Derrida's chosen texts are those which more or less explicitly *thematize* the deconstructive logic at work within them. Thus Plato constructs an elaborate mythology around the privileged themes of speech and writing, presence and absence, philosophic truth and poetic unreason. In Rousseau likewise the 'logic of the supplement' is instanced by pursuing a whole series of interrelated themes.[14] These include the instances of nature versus culture; of 'natural' sexuality versus the homoerotic; or the innocence of primitive speech as opposed to the 'dangerous supplement' of writing. What is aimed at is undoubtedly – as Gasché would argue – a deconstructive movement which works to undo such loaded oppositions, not merely as 'themes' in this text or that but as manifest throughout the discourse of western tradition. Nevertheless it must be recognized that much of the force of Derrida's arguments comes of his fastening upon texts which obsessively (if unconsciously) *foreground* the means of their own deconstruction.

The same applies to those exemplary 'allegories of reading' which de Man discovers in the texts of Rousseau, Nietzsche and Proust.[15] Let us grant – as de Man repeatedly insists – that these are *not* interpretative readings of individual works, but cases of a generalized textual predicament which drives a wedge between logic and rhetoric, sense and intent, 'constative' and 'performative' aspects of language. Still it is the case that his texts are so chosen as to thematize the rhetorical blind-spots and perplexities which solicit a deconstructive reading. Thus Nietzsche, as canny rhetorician, provides explicit leads for deconstructing his own operative tropes; while Rousseau foregrounds the confessional or truth-telling mode which his own skills of narrative contrivance will effectively place in question. Gasché's attempt to beat the bounds of a rigorous deconstruction runs up against very real problems here. It may be – as he argues – a facile misunderstanding which seeks to blur the line between deconstruction and those themes of 'self-reflexive' textuality that literary critics delight to uncover. Yet this very distinction can be seen to rest on an act of presumptive foreclosure, a structured opposition which in turn lies open to deconstructive treatment.

The terms of this exclusive and systematized repression are evident in the passage from Gasché quoted above. Deconstruction must aim at 'textuality as such', rather than interpreting the 'self-reflexive' text on the grounds of its 'historical and thematic determination'. This presupposes, firstly, that a rigid demarcation holds between these two possible lines of approach; secondly, that one of them – *echt*-deconstruction – effectively excludes the other. Excludes it, that is, while at the same time making it possible, since – as Gasché contends – 'textuality as such' is the primordial phenomenon properly aimed at beyond all the secondary 'strata' of self-reflexivity.

This contention, for all its purist-Derridean claims, runs counter to the deconstructionist principle which would question all such exclusive or privileged orders of valorization. I would argue, contrary to Gasché, that deconstruction is always and everywhere involved in the business of textual 'interpretation', even if it works to overthrow conventional ideas of interpretative relevance and point. The difference of approach between say de Man and J. Hillis Miller is not to be explained by categorizing the one as an authentic (first-order or 'textual') deconstructor and the other as a picker-up of handy deconstructionist 'themes'. It is rather that de Man practises a different *mode* of deconstruction, one aimed chiefly toward aberrant figures of textual implication which bear on his own special interests as conceptual rhetorician or Nietzschean demystifier of tropes. Miller finds the same strange phenomena at work, but manifest on a larger (narrative-thematic) scale. He discovers, that is to say, metaphors of narrative doubling and 'uncanny' repetition which tend to undermine the surface plausibilities of nineteenth-century 'realist' fiction.[16]

Gasché would object that such 'self-reflexive' readings are merely a facile displacement, for literary-critical ends, of the primary work of textual deconstruction. In fact, as I have argued, this distinction breaks down as soon as one asks how deconstruction can possibly get a hold on any text without pursuing those elements of self-reflexivity which foreground its textual constitution. An obvious example would be Derrida's treatment of Poe's 'The purloined letter'.[17] The tale becomes an 'allegory of reading' in the sense that its themes (of concealment, circulation and reciprocal error) are taken to signify the textual predicament of all interpretation. The letter – elusive object of Dupin's quest – becomes an instance or metaphor of that 'floating signifier' which circulates beyond reach of un-equivocal meaning or truth. The story is thus staged deconstruc-tively as a narrative working-out of the problems which beset understanding when it strives to master the play of textual dissemination. Such a reading works back, as it were allegori-cally, from narrative theme to its 'self-reflexive' import, and thence to a standpoint of generalized reflection on the para-doxes of representation. It thus stands opposed to Gasché's strict demand that deconstruction should bypass – or rigorously pre-empt – the 'thematic' and 'self-reflexive' strata of texts.

Derrida's essay takes issue with a celebrated reading of 'The purloined letter' based on one of Lacan's seminars and subse-quently published in his *Ecrits*.[18] According to Derrida, Lacan has ignored or repressed the 'disseminating' play of the text, determined as he is to treat it as a virtual *mise en scène* of Lacanian psychoanalysis. From a deconstructive viewpoint this amounts to yet another defensive retreat in the face of textuality, an appeal to some privileged order of truth (the psychoanalytic) which escapes the subversive effects of writing and *differance*. Yet Derrida himself – as Barbara Johnson shrewdly notes – cannot help but fill in the 'absent' themes (castration, sexuality, writing) which Lacan is supposedly constrained to ignore. As Johnson explains it:

> Derrida, in his effort to right (write) Lacan's wrongs, can, on a certain level, only repeat them ... the rectification of a

previous injustice somehow irresistibly dictates the filling in of a blank which then becomes the new injustice.[19]

The result is what Johnson wittily calls a game of critical 'one-downmanship'. Theory is caught out by the play of rhetorical signification which continues to circulate beyond its control or conceptual grasp.

Gasché is fully justified in arguing that this condition of non-recuperable meaning is outside the terms of any purely 'thematic' reading. Still it is the case that neither Lacan, Derrida nor Johnson would have been in a position to broach their specific *differances* had the tale not provided a peculiarly apt and productive starting-point. The very title 'The purloined letter' lends itself to deconstructive treatment, whether in Lacanian terms (the 'insistence of the letter' as agent of desire), or as Derrida would read it, a staging of endlessly deferred signification. The *theme* of Poe's tale is developed into a deconstructive allegory of reading none the less cogent for its analogical basis. To exclude or devalue such 'thematic' readings as abuses of deconstruction is to set aside virtually everything so far achieved in its name.

At root of Gasché's argument is a move to validate philosophy (= purist deconstruction) as opposed to the derivative practice of literary criticism. 'Only from the basis of this philosophical insight [the absence of the referent] can the operation of deconstruction, drawn with all possible logical rigor, begin.'[20] On the same page Gasché contrasts the 'genuinely philosophical' with the merely interpretative uses of deconstruction. But this is to confuse two separate issues. Deconstruction belongs to 'philosophy' – or to a certain self-image of philosophic rigour – in so far as it aims at textual effects beyond the compass of any purely thematic interpretation. On the other hand this gives no warrant for assuming some kind of *a priori* incompatibility between the purposes of deconstruction strictly conceived and those of a literary criticism itself fully apprised of deconstructionist principles. Gasché's argument thus falls prey to a reductive one-sided valorization which equates intellectual rigour with purity of *philosophic* motive. He is in danger of ignoring what Derrida and de Man most insistently urge: the need to think beyond such typecast institutional categories as those of 'philosophy', 'literature' and 'literary criticism'. For de Man especially, deconstruction bids fair to overthrow the age-old prejudice that elevates philosophic truth and reason at the expense of literary feigning. It then becomes a matter of asking, like de Man, why philosophy has so long refused to avail itself of those techniques for rhetorical demystification developed by literary critics.

The reader will no doubt be aware by now that this rejoinder to Gasché is partly by way of pre-emptive self-defence. The chapters in this volume – especially those on Kierkegaard, Wittgenstein and Austin – are examples of deconstruction in what Gasché would doubtless call a 'thematic' and hence non-rigorous form. They fasten, that is to say, on those moments of textual doubt or indecision where philosophy glimpses, and forthwith represses, its own 'literary' status. Thus Kierkegaard essays the limits of fictional (mis)representation in the interests of finally closing the brackets on literature and conveying some ultimate, authentic truth. Wittgenstein's phonocentric philosophy of language-games comes up against insistent metaphors of an alien, arbitrary writing; while Austin strives to exclude or marginalize 'deviant' (literary) speech-act instances which nevertheless serve to structure the very logic of his argument. It is my argument that these texts contrive to highlight the problems of writing and fictionality even as they attempt to contain or repress such topics. And this means in turn that the most rewarding texts for deconstructive treatment are those which more or less explicitly *thematize* their own problematical status.

My essay on Kripke perhaps comes nearest to satisfying Gasché's stringent demands. That is, it has to do with issues of logic and language, meaning and reference which inherently resist translation out of their own clearly defined conceptual idiom. Nevertheless it is my contention that Kripke's particular form of philosophical rigour is at certain points open to a reading – a textual-deconstructionist reading – which would question its putative grounding in a schema of logical necessity immune from such interrogation. And this comes about through attending to the *rhetoric* of Kripke's text, its strategic resort to illustrative metaphors and fictions. Such is his appeal to an originary 'baptism' of reference, located in some purely hypothetical past event but serving to legitimate Kripke's whole argument for the necessary link between naming and sense.

This is not to deny the possibility or point of 'philosophical rigour' as applied to the work of deconstruction. Rather, it is to argue that such value-terms need to be revised – or provisionally suspended – in the face of those conceptual blind-spots which deconstruction so persistently reveals. I would furthermore claim that these essays are none the less 'rigorous' for their dealing in thematic and self-reflexive aspects of the philosophic writings in question. Certainly they find ample warrant – as I have urged – in the currently exemplary practices of Derrida and de Man. Deconstruction cannot finally sever all ties with the business of 'interpreting' texts, however far-reaching its challenge to received ideas of that activity.

Appendix:
on Henning Fenger's 'Kierkegaard: the myths and their origins'

Since completing the chapter on Kierkegaard my attention has been drawn (as they say) to a recent study by the Danish scholar Henning Fenger (*Kierkegaard: the myths and their origins*, trans. George C. Schoolfield, New Haven: Yale University Press, 1980). It is a combative book, briskly polemical in tone and aimed at demolishing most of what passes for standard – Fenger would say 'pious' – Kierkegaard scholarship. His approach is by no means theoretical, much less deconstructionist; but his argument presses toward conclusions which do, in a sense, bear out what I have been arguing here. Fenger questions the assumption – taken on trust from Kierkegaard by his faithful interpreters – that the 'aesthetic' works are merely stages on the path to a commanding religious perspective which totally subsumes and transcends them. This standpoint relies on the foregone conclusion that Kierkegaard left fiction behind once and for all when he broke with his various distancing pseudonyms and elected to write in authentic (religious) good faith. In fact, Fenger argues, there was no such decisive shift, or at least no evidence, in the texts and sources, which would serve to confirm such a view. It is a matter of choice – of 'existential' commitment – whether or not one believes what Kierkegaard had to say about the motives and structuring intent of his authorship as a whole. Fenger, for his part, chooses flatly not to believe, and builds an elaborate scholarly case in support of that refusal.

His argument comes down to the central claim that Kierkegaard's followers have systematically (if unconsciously) ignored and suppressed the more embarrassing ambiguities in his writing. That is to say, they have accepted his spiritual auto-biography – the 'leap into faith' and its consequent retrospective slant on his life and work – as a matter of straightforward authentic truth. Fenger provides plentiful evidence of the exclusions, distortions and selective emphases which have gone into the making of this Kierkegaard 'myth'. Most strikingly, he argues that Kierkegaard himself laid elaborate false trails for future scholarship by concealing or (apparently) falsifying the dates of composition for certain crucial documents. As a result, Kierkegaard research 'went down the wrong track at the outset', and devoted itself to bolstering up a myth of authenticity all the more beguiling for its truth to Kierkegaard's manifest intent.

Fenger denies that his purpose in all this is to cut Kierkegaard down to size, or to cast him as a posturing charlatan successfully imposing his own bad faith on later generations of simple-minded scholars. Kierkegaard, he says, 'like anyone else ... had the right to suppress, rewrite, misrepresent, distort, erase, destroy, and lead astray, and to arrange the interpretation of his life and his works. In precisely whatever way he pleased' (p.xiii). Behind his appearance of prosecuting zeal Fenger is raising the cardinal question: how can the line be drawn, in Kierkegaard's writing, between faith, fiction and the strategies of authorship designed to dramatize their relation?

Fenger finds this question posed most acutely in the letters and papers – reputedly 'authentic' – which concern Kierke-gaard's broken engagement to Regine Olsen. They constitute, on his submission, a cruel and even sadistic game with the girl's affections, a species of elaborately staged melodrama which Kierkegaard plotted as a means of disguising his own psychosexual inadequacy. As Fenger reads them, the letters belong to the 'aesthetic' or literary side of Kierkegaard's produc-tion, if indeed there remains any need for that category when all his writings can be argued to partake of it in some degree. His treatment of Regine loses its claim to ethical (or religious) self-determination and begins to look more like an uncanny re-enactment of the tactics employed by Johnannes the Seducer in Volume 1 of *Either/Or*. It can also be seen – Fenger argues – as an outcome of Kierkegaard's early involvement with that

German tradition of romanticized love and despair epitomized in Friedrich Schlegel's *Lucinde* and, pre-eminently, in Goethe's *Werther*. These sources point back in turn to the eighteenth-century French line of intimate and libertine fiction which includes *Les Liaisons Dangereuses* and – at the limit – Sade's *La Philosophie dans le Boudoir*. It is here, Fenger suggests, in the confused twilight zone between fiction and confessional truth, that Kierkegaard's self-dramatizing treatment of Regine finds its closest analogues.

The thrust of Fenger's arguments is deconstructionist in outcome if not in name or allegiance. He reads the narrative of Kierkegaard's life – both the first-hand texts and the secondary scholarship – as, for all we can know, a product of fictional contriving, to be tested against the evidence at every point. Of course such 'evidence' – dates, circumstances, factual corroborations – would find small room in purely deconstructionist readings such as Derrida or de Man on Rousseau. Their object is to show how the text itself gives rise to figural or fictive possibilities at odds with its own confessional, truth-telling ethos. Nevertheless the lines of argument have this much in common: that they both set out to problematize the normative assumption which construes narrative meaning in terms of some guiding teleology or deep-lying purposive intent. Fenger locates this meaning in Kierkegaard's desire – and that of his interpreters – to discover an end-point of religious justification which serves to transume and revalue everything pertaining to the 'aesthetic' stage. To question this authorized version is to demythologize Kierkegaard's life and works, since the two are intertwined in such a complex and – as Fenger would argue – such a deeply contradictory way.

The upshot is no less far-reaching than de Man's description of Rousseau's *Confessions* as a textual machine with an infinite capacity for creating (and excusing) fictitious guilt. Thus, for Fenger, the breaking of Kierkegaard's engagement is not – as orthodox scholars would have it – the act of a self-possessed consciousness already in dialectical pursuit of a higher religious wisdom. Rather, he argues, the crisis was rudely precipitated by Kierkegaard's learning of Regine's engagement to another man (whom she subsequently married). Take this fact into account and it becomes, as Fenger says, altogether understandable from a psychological point of view that he now leaps into faith and glorifies his 'sacrifice': his renunciation of Regine becomes a religious act in the service of higher powers. The existential choices are always easier if other people make them for us.   (p.219)

Fenger will acknowledge no animus toward Kierkegaard; only toward the 'learned men, the scribes, docents male and female' who have taken him faithfully at his word. A 'healthy scepticism' is the requisite attitude for beginning to sort out just how much belongs to fiction and the realm of aesthetic self-concealment.

De Man's deconstructionist reading of Nietzsche brings him to the point where philosophy turns out to be 'an endless reflection on its own destruction at the hands of literature'. My own reading of Kierkegaard suggests that a similar possibility haunts the very texts in which he claims to have renounced 'literature' and taken the leap into authentic religious self-knowledge. Of course there is no question of seizing on Fenger's evidence – the crucial misdatings, 'literary' sources, contrived alibis – as if somehow to prove the case for deconstructing Kierkegaard. That case has to stand on a rigorous reading of the texts, a reading alive to the non-coincidence of ethos and meaning, strategy and sense. Fenger's argument has to do with problems specific to Kierkegaard scholarship and criticism; deconstruction is properly concerned with issues of language and representation beyond any single interpretative instance.

All the same there is a striking convergence between Fenger's principled scepticism – a matter of scholarly scruple – and the outcome of a deconstructionist reading. It emerges most clearly in his chapter on the *Letters*, where the constant intermingling of fact and fiction, private and 'literary' reference, creates a baffling textual *clair-obscur*. Fenger's suggestion – advanced with copious supporting argument – is that we read these letters as the remnant of a failed literary project, an epistolary *Bildungsroman* in the Goethean tradition. More specifically, the aim was to create a new genre, that of the Danish novella, treating philosophically of sentimental themes. The reader is free to reject this proposal (the 'fiction theory'), perhaps on ethical or religious-doctrinal grounds. But the price of keeping faith with the Kierkegaard myth (as Fenger regards it) is a textual and scholarly conundrum of impossible proportions. Of the arguments for accepting it:

> The fall, the visit to the bordello, the irregular taking of Holy Communion, the family curse, the death of the Kierkegaard offspring before or at the latest in their thirty-fourth year (the age of Christ at his death), the thorn in the flesh, the secret note, and many other tidbits . . ., all of this sinks back into the Romantic tradition itself. (p.231)

It may be that the 'existential reader' has a right to believe or disbelieve the myth handed down by Kierkegaard's loyal disciples. In the same way, deconstruction has to acknowledge that 'naïve' (or rhetorically unsophisticated) readings must continue to exercise a certain persuasive charm against the rigours of textual analysis. Yet there is, of course, a limit to this even-handed attitude. It is clear that neither Fenger nor de Man entertains any serious doubt as to which kind of reading constitutes present good faith on the interpreter's part.

Notes

Preface

1 I. A. Richards, *Science and Poetry* (London: Psyche Miniatures, No.1, 1926).

2 See especially Paul de Man, 'The epistemology of metaphor', *Critical Inquiry*, vol. V (1978), pp. 13–30.

3 Terry Eagleton, *Walter Benjamin, or towards a revolutionary criticism* (London: New Left Books, 1981), p. 132.

4 Paul de Man, *Allegories of Reading: figural language in Rousseau, Nietzsche, Rilke and Proust* (New Haven and London: Yale University Press, 1979), p. 115.

5 Jacques Derrida, *Of Grammatology*, trans. Gayatri Chakravorty Spivak (Baltimore and London: Johns Hopkins University Press, 1977), p. 24.

6 For an argument against the literary-interpretative uses of deconstruction, see Rodolphe Gasché, 'Deconstruction as criticism', *Glyph*, vol. VI (1979), pp. 177–215.

7 W. V. O. Quine, 'Two dogmas of empiricism' in T. M. Olshewski (ed.), *Problems in the Philosophy of Language* (New York: Holt, Rinehart and Winston, 1969), pp. 398–417.

8 W. V. O. Quine, 'Things and their place in theories' in Quine, *Theories and Things* (Cambridge, Mass. and London: Harvard University Press, 1981), pp. 1–23; p. 1.

9 Israel Scheffler, *Beyond the Letter: a philosophical inquiry into ambiguity, vagueness and metaphor in language* (London: Routledge & Kegan Paul, 1979).

10 ibid., p. 8.

11 ibid., p. 9

12 ibid., p. xi.

13 See Nelson Goodman, 'On likeness of meaning' and 'On some

differences about meaning' in Goodman, *Problems and Projects* (Indianapolis and New York: Bobbs-Merrill, 1972), pp. 221–30 and 231–8.

14 Scheffler, *Beyond the Letter*, p. 23

15 ibid., p. 9.

16 Derrida, op. cit., p. 46.

17 Scheffler, *Beyond the Letter*, p. 6.

18 ibid., p. 129.

19 ibid., p. 78.

Chapter 1

1 Ferdinand de Saussure, *Course in General Linguistics*, trans. Wade Baskin (London: Fontana/Collins, 1974).

2 Jacques Derrida, *Of Grammatology*, trans. Gayatri Chakravorty Spivak (Baltimore and London: Johns Hopkins University Press, 1977).

3 Quoted by Spivak in her Preface to *Of Grammatology*, p. xxii.

4 See Christopher Norris, *Deconstruction: theory and practice* (London: Methuen, 1982).

5 See Jacques Derrida, *The Archaeology of the Frivolous: reading Condillac*, trans. John P. Leavey (Pittsburgh: Duquesne University Press, 1980).

6 See for instance Jacques Derrida, *'Speech and Phenomena' and other essays on Husserl's theory of signs*, trans. David B. Allison (Evanston, Ill.: Northwestern University Press, 1973).

7 Richard Rorty, *Philosophy and the Mirror of Nature* (Oxford: Basil Blackwell, 1980), p. 12.

8 ibid., p. 143.

9 See Richard Rorty, 'Philosophy as a kind of writing', *New Literary History*, vol. X (1978), pp. 141–60. Reprinted in Rorty, *The Consequences of Pragmatism* (Brighton: Harvester Press, 1982), pp. 90–109.

10 Gilbert Ryle, *The Concept of Mind* (London: Hutchinson, 1949).

11 Paul de Man, *Allegories of Reading: fictional language in Rousseau, Nietzsche, Rilke and Proust* (New Haven: Yale University Press, 1979), p. 10.

12 ibid., p. 131.

13 Gilbert Ryle, 'Philosophical arguments' in James B. Hartman (ed.), *Philosophy of Recent Times*, vol. II (New York and London: McGraw Hill, 1967), pp. 489–503.

14 ibid., p. 491.

15 ibid., p. 493.

16 ibid., p. 492.

17 Jacques Derrida, 'Genesis and structure' in *Writing and Difference*, trans. Alan Bass (London: Routledge & Kegan Paul, 1978), pp. 154–68; p. 159.

18 ibid., p. 160.

19 ibid., p. 162.

20 Gilbert Ryle, review of Martin Farber's *The Foundations of Phenomenology* in Ryle, *Collected Papers*, vol. I (London: Hutchinson, 1971), pp. 215–24; p. 221.

21 Gilbert Ryle, 'Heidegger's *Sein und Zeit*' in Ryle, *Collected Papers*, vol. I, pp. 197–214; p. 211.

22 See Jacques Derrida, *Spurs: Nietzsche's Styles*, trans. Barbara Harlow (Chicago and London: University of Chicago Press, 1979).

23 Gilbert Ryle, 'Letters and syllables in Plato' in Ryle, *Collected Papers*, vol. I, pp. 54–71; p. 64.

24 See Jacques Derrida, *Dissemination*, trans. Barbara Johnson (London: Athlone Press, 1982).

25 Ryle, 'Letters and syllables in Plato', p. 57.

26 ibid., p. 60.

27 See Derrida, *Of Grammatology*, particularly pp. 1–93.

28 Ryle, 'Letters and syllables in Plato', p. 68.

29 See Derrida, *Of Grammatology*, pp. 30–73.

30 Ryle, 'Letters and syllables in Plato', p. 60.

31 See Jacques Derrida, 'Signature Event Context', *Glyph*, vol. I (Baltimore and London: Johns Hopkins University Press, 1977), pp. 172–97; also John R. Searle, 'Reiterating the differences', *Glyph*, vol. I, pp. 198–208; and Derrida, 'Limited inc abc', *Glyph*, vol. II (1977), pp. 162–254.

32 Derrida, 'Limited inc abc', p. 254.

Chapter 2

1 Ludwig Wittgenstein, *Philosophical Investigations*, trans. G.E.M. Anscombe (Oxford: Blackwell, 1963).

2 ibid., p. 47e.

3 See for instance Charles Altieri, 'Wittgenstein on consciousness and language: a challenge to Derridean theory', *Modern Language Notes*, vol. XCI (1976), pp. 1397–423.

4 Wittgenstein, *Philosophical Investigations*, p. vii.

5 See particularly Jacques Derrida, *Of Grammatology*, trans. Gayatri Chakravorty Spivak (Baltimore and London: Johns Hopkins University Press, 1977).

6 On metaphor in the text of philosophy (with particular reference to Locke), see Paul de Man, 'The epistemology of metaphor', *Critical*

Inquiry, vol. V (1978), pp. 13–30.

7 Wittgenstein, *Philosophical Investigations*, p. 46e.

8 ibid., p. 216e

9 ibid., p. 222e

10 ibid., p. 223e.

11 ibid., p. 216e.

12 Derrida, *Of Grammatology*, p. lxxv.

13 Wittgenstein, *Philosophical Investigations*, p. 214e.

14 ibid., p. 64e.

15 ibid., p. 215e.

16 ibid., p. 128e.

17 ibid., p. 82e.

18 For a general account of Derrida's writings, see Christopher Norris, *Deconstruction: theory and practice* (London: Methuen, 1982).

19 Wittgenstein, *Philosophical Inventions*, p. 67e.

20 ibid., p. 68e.

21 ibid., p. 218e.

22 Derrida, *Of Grammatology*, p. 160.

23 ibid., p. 98.

24 ibid., p. 98.

25 Wittgenstein, *Philosophical Investigations*, p. 45e.

26 Gilbert Ryle, *The Concept of Mind* (London: Hutchinson, 1949).

27 Wittgenstein, *Philosophical Investigations*, p. 220e.

28 Jacques Derrida, *'Speech and Phenomena' and other essays on Husserl's theory of signs*, trans. David B. Allison (Evanston, Ill.: Northwestern University Press, 1973).

29 See for instance Edmund Husserl, *Cartesian Meditations*, trans. Dorian Cairns (The Hague: Martinus Nijhoff, 1960).

30 Derrida, *'Speech and Phenomena'*, pp. 20–1.

31 Wittgenstein, *Philosophical Investigations*, p. 68e.

32 ibid.

33 ibid., p. 220e.

34 See the essay 'Differance' in Derrida, *'Speech and Phenomena'*, pp. 129–60.

35 Wittgenstein, *Philosophical Investigations*, p. 69e.

36 ibid., p. 69e.

37 ibid., pp. 69–70e.

38 Jacques Derrida, 'Plato's pharmacy', in *Dissemination*, trans. Barbara Johnson (London: Athlone Press, 1982), pp. 61–171.

39 ibid., pp. 95–6.

40 Wittgenstein, *Philosophical Investigations*, p. 49e.

41 ibid., p. 47e.

Chapter 3

1 Roderick Firth, 'Austin's argument from illusion' in K. T. Fann (ed.), *A Symposium on J. L. Austin* (London: Routledge & Kegan Paul, 1969), pp. 254–66; p. 254.

2 J. O. Urmson, 'Austin's philosophy' in Fann, op. cit., pp. 22–32; p. 25.

3 Jacques Derrida, 'Signature Event Context', *Glyph*, vol. I (1977), pp. 172–97.

4 J. L. Austin, *How To Do Things With Words* (London: Oxford University Press, 1962), p. 22.

5 See especially Jacques Derrida, *Of Grammatology*, trans. Gayatri Chakravorty Spivak (Baltimore and London: Johns Hopkins University Press, 1977).

6 John R. Searle, 'Reiterating the differences', *Glyph*, vol. I (1977), pp. 198–208.

7 A point made by Barbara Johnson in her essay 'Mallarmé and Austin'. See Johnson, *The Critical Difference: essays in the rhetoric of contemporary reading* (Baltimore: Johns Hopkins University Press, 1980), pp. 52–66.

8 G. J. Warnock, 'Saturday mornings' in Isaiah Berlin *et al.*, *Essays on J. L. Austin* (London: Oxford University Press, 1973), pp. 31–45; p. 43.

9 Austin, *How To Do Things With Words*, p. 61.

10 Warnock, 'Saturday mornings', p. 45.

11 See Jacques Derrida, 'Limited inc abc', *Glyph*, vol. II (1977), pp. 162–254.

12 See Plato, *The Phaedrus and Letters VII and VIII*, trans. Walter Hamilton (Harmondsworth: Penguin, 1973).

13 Sir Philip Sidney, 'Defence of Poesie' in G. Gregory Smith (ed.), *Elizabethan Critical Essays* (London, 1924).

14 Jacques Derrida, 'Plato's pharmacy' in *Dissemination*, trans. Barbara Johnson (London: Athlone Press, 1982), pp. 61–171.

15 Austin, *How To Do Things With Words*, p. 75.

16 ibid., p. 65.

17 J. L. Austin, 'A plea for excuses' in *Philosophical Papers* (London: Oxford University Press, 1961), pp. 123–52; p. 133.

18 J. O. Urmson, contribution to 'A symposium on Austin's method' in Fann, *A symposium on J. L. Austin*, pp. 76–86; p. 79.

19 Austin, *How To Do Things With Words*, p. 92n.

20 ibid., p. 102.

21 ibid., p. 96.

22 ibid., p. 97.

23 See for instance Wayne C. Booth, *The Rhetoric of Fiction* (Chicago and London: University of Chicago Press, 1961); Seymour Chatman,

Story and Discourse (Ithaca, New York: Cornell University Press, 1978). The field is too wide to permit of any adequate survey here; an up-to-date bibliography may be found in Horst Ruthrof, *The Reader's Construction of Narrative* (London: Routledge & Kegan Paul, 1981).

24 Colin MacCabe, *James Joyce and the Revolution of the Word* (London: Macmillan, 1978), pp. 13–14.

25 Austin, *How To Do Things With Words*, p. 150.

26 ibid.,p. 66.

27 Austin, 'A plea for excuses', p. 128.

28 ibid., p. 140.

29 Austin, *How To Do Things With Words*, p. 55.

30 Derrida, 'Plato's Pharmacy' in *Dissemination*, pp. 61–171.

31 Derrida, '. . . That dangerous supplement' in *Of Grammatology*, pp. 141–64.

32 C. G. New, 'A plea for linguistics' in Fann, op. cit., pp. 148–65; p. 150.

33 Austin, 'A plea for excuses', p. 130.

34 See for instance C. W. K Mundle, *A Critique of Linguistic Philosophy* (Oxford: Clarendon Press, 1970) and Keith Graham, *J. L. Austin: a critique of ordinary-language philosophy* (Brighton: Harvester Press, 1977).

35 For instance Ernest Gellner, *Words and Things* (London: Gollancz, 1959).

36 Austin, 'A plea for excuses', p. 130.

37 ibid., p. 131.

38 ibid., p. 130.

39 ibid., p. 131.

40 Walter Cerf, critical review of *How To Do Things With Words* in Fann, op. cit., pp. 351–79.

41 ibid., p. 366.

42 Austin, *How To Do Things With Words*, p. 56.

43 Austin, 'Pretending' in *Philosophical Papers*, pp. 201–19; p. 215.

44 ibid., p. 217.

45 Shakespeare, *As You Like It*, Act III, scene iii, lines 17–18. The Clown's speech rings changes on the word and includes (in the Folio text) both spellings: 'No truly: for the truest poetrie is the most faining, and Lovers are given to Poetrie: and what they sweare in Poetrie, may be saide as Lovers, they do feigne.' A Variorum footnote has it that this was subsequently the poet Waller's 'courtly apology to Charles II for having praised Cromwell'.

Chapter 4

1 Kierkegaard, *The Point of View for My Work as an Author*, trans. Walter Lowrie (London and New York: Oxford University Press, 1939), p. 91.

2 Kierkegaard, *The Point of View*, p. 12.

3 ibid., p. 18.

4 ibid., p. 18.

5 ibid., p. 155.

6 ibid., p. 90.

7 ibid., p. 90.

8 See Paul de Man, *Allegories of Reading: figural language in Rousseau, Nietzsche, Rilke and Proust* (New Haven and London: Yale University Press, 1979).

9 Kierkegaard, *Either/Or*, vols. I and II, trans. David F. Swenson and Lillian Marvin Swenson (New Jersey: Princeton University Press, 1971).

10 Kierkegaard, *The Point of View*, p. 17.

11 See especially his powerfully argued riposte to deconstruction in the closing chapter of Harold Bloom, *Wallace Stevens: the poems of our climate* (Ithaca, New York and London: Cornell University Press, 1977).

12 Kierkegaard, *The Point of View*, p. 1/.

13 ibid., p. 8.

14 Jacques Derrida, *Spurs: Nietzsche's Styles*, trans. Barbara Harlow (Chicago and London: University of Chicago Press, 1979), p. 89.

15 ibid., p. 97.

16 Kierkegaard, *The Point of View*, p. 83.

17 ibid., p. 83.

18 On the general topic of narrative viewpoint and strategy, see Wayne C. Booth, *The Rhetoric of Fiction* (Chicago and London: University of Chicago Press, 1961). For a critique of their specific ideological implications, see Colin MacCabe, *James Joyce and the Revolution of the Word* (London: Macmillan, 1978), especially pp. 13–38.

19 Kierkegaard, *The Point of View*, p. 83.

20 Paul de Man, *Allegories of Reading*, p. 280.

21 ibid., p. 293.

22 ibid., p. 293.

23 ibid., p. 279.

24 ibid., p. 299.

25 Kierkegaard, *The Point of View*, p. 17.

26 See for instance J. L. Austin, *How To Do Things With Words* (London: Oxford University Press, 1963) and John R. Searle, *Speech Acts: an essay in the philosophy of language* (Cambridge: Cambridge University

Press, 1972).

27 Paul de Man, *Allegories of Reading*, p. 282.

28 ibid., p. 300.

29 ibid., p. 131.

30 For much useful comment on Kierkegaard's relationship to Hegel, see Mark C. Taylor, *Kierkegaard's Pseudonymous Authorship* (New Jersey: Princeton University Press, 1975).

31 Paul de Man, *Allegories of Reading*, p. 298.

32 For the passage in question see Rousseau, *Oeuvres Complètes, Les Confessions, autres textes autobiographiques*, ed. Bernard Gagnebin and Marcel Raymond (Paris: Gallimard, 1959), vol. I, pp. 85–7. In the most convenient English translation (London: Dent, 1931) it appears on pp. 74–7.

33 Paul de Man, *Allegories of Reading*, p. 285.

34 ibid., p. 285.

35 Kierkegaard, *Johnannes Climacus or, De Omnibus Dubitandum Est and a Sermon*, trans, T. H. Croxall (Stanford, California: Stanford University Press, 1967), pp. 148–9.

36 Paul de Man, *Allegories of Reading*, p. 294.

37 ibid., p. 130.

38 Kierkegaard, *The Point of View*, p. 20.

39 As translated by Gayatri Chakravorty Spivak in her Preface to Jacques Derrida, *Of Grammatology* (Baltimore and London: Johns Hopkins University Press, 1977), p. xxii.

40 Kierkegaard, *The Last Years: Journals, 1853–5*, ed. and trans. Ronald Gregor Smith (London: Collins/Fontana, 1968), p. 198–9.

41 ibid., p. 200.

42 ibid., p. 201.

43 For a detailed and informative discussion of these differences, see Taylor, *Kierkegaard's Pseudonymous Authorship*, pp. 11–37.

Chapter 5

1 Terry Eagleton, *Criticism and Ideology* (London: New Left Books, 1976).

2 Louis Althusser, *For Marx*, trans. Ben Brewster (Harmondsworth: Allen Lane, 1969), p. 39.

3 ibid., p. 251.

4 See E. P. Thompson, *The Poverty of Theory and other essays* (London: Merlin, 1978).

5 Terry Eagleton, *Walter Benjamin, or towards a revolutionary criticism* (London: New Left Books, 1981).

6 Walter Benjamin, 'Theses on the philosophy of history' in

Illuminations, ed. Hannah Arendt (London: Fontana, 1973), p. 259.

7 Walter Benjamin, *Charles Baudelaire: a lyric poet in the era of high capitalism*, trans. Harry Zohn (London: New Left Books, 1973). See also Benjamin's essay 'On some motifs in Baudelaire', translated in *Illuminations*.

8 Walter Benjamin, 'The work of art in the age of mechanical reproduction' in *Illuminations*, pp. 219–53.

9 Walter Benjamin, 'The author as producer' in *Understanding Brecht*, trans. Anna Bostock (London: New Left Books, 1973), p. 98.

10 George Steiner, introduction to Benjamin's *The Origin of German Tragic Drama* (London: New Left Books, 1977), p. 24.

11 William Empson, *Some Versions of Pastoral* (Harmondsworth: Penguin, 1966), p. 12.

12 ibid., p. 22.

13 Walter Benjamin, 'Conversations with Brecht' in *Understanding Brecht*, p. 110.

14 Empson, op. cit., p.23.

15 Quoted in Fredric Jameson, *Marxism and Form* (New Jersey: Princeton University Press, 1971), p. 61n.

16 ibid., p. 77.

17 Walter Benjamin, *The Origins of German Tragic Drama*, trans. John Osborne (London: New Left Books, 1977).

18 ibid., p. 29.

19 ibid., p. 231.

20 ibid., p. 229.

21 See for instance Carol Jacobs, 'Walter Benjamin: image of Proust', *Modern Language Notes*, 89 (1971), pp. 910–32.

22 Argued most forcefully in Jacques Derrida, *Of Grammatology*, trans. Gayatri Chakravorty Spivak (Baltimore and London: Johns Hopkins University Press, 1977).

23 See for instance Paul de Man, *Allegories of Reading: figural Language in Rousseau, Nietzsche, Rilke and Proust* (New Haven and London: Yale University Press, 1979).

24 Paul de Man, *Blindness and Insight: essays in the rhetoric of contemporary criticism* (London: Oxford University Press, 1971), p. 29.

25 Walter Benjamin, *The Origins of German Tragic Drama*, p. 160.

26 ibid., pp. 224–5.

27 Eagleton, *Walter Benjamin*, p. 132.

28 ibid., p. 115.

29 Walter Benjamin, *The Origins of German Tragic Drama*, p. 235.

Chapter 6

1 A. O. J. Lovejoy, 'On the discrimination of Romanticisms', *PMLA*, vol. XXXIX (1974), pp. 229–53.

2 For a useful collective statement of the Yale-deconstructionist outlook, see Geoffrey Hartman, Harold Bloom, Paul de Man *et al.*, *Deconstruction and Criticism* (London: Routledge & Kegan Paul, 1979).

3 For the substance of Eliot's 'case' against Shelley – and the ethos of Romanticism generally – see T. S. Eliot, *The Use of Poetry and the Use of Criticism* (London: Faber & Faber, 1933). A powerful riposte from the adversary camp may be found in Harold Bloom, *Shelley's Mythmaking* (New Haven: Yale University Press, 1959).

4 In this connection, see my remarks on Allen Tate and R. P. Blackmur in Christopher Norris, *Deconstruction: theory and practice* (London: Methuen, 1982), pp. 13–14.

5 See particularly Geoffrey Hartman, 'The interpreter: a self-analysis', in Hartman, *The Fate of Reading* (Chicago: University of Chicago Press, 1975), pp. 3–19.

6 Paul de Man, *Allegories of Reading: figural language in Rousseau, Nietzsche, Rilke and Proust* (New Haven and London: Yale University Press, 1979).

7 See Norris, *Deconstruction: theory and practice*.

8 Paul de Man, *Allegories of Reading*, p. 115.

9 ibid., p. 60.

10 Hartman, 'The interpreter: a self-analysis', p. 17.

11 For Coleridge's account of the dream, see vol. I of the *Complete Poetical Works*, ed. Ernest Hartley Coleridge (Oxford: Oxford University Press, 1912), pp. 295–6.

12 Coleridge, *Biographia Literaria*, ed. J. Shawcross (2 vols, Oxford: Oxford University Press, 1907). See especially vol. I, pp. 202ff. It is intriguing to note that Wimsatt and Brooks – though arguing from an 'old' New Critical position remote from a critic like de Man – offer the following remarks about Coleridge's philosophic quandary:

> A confusion between poetic theory as operative in poems and poetic theory as their stated content is most often a feat of the historian and critic, rather than of the original theorist or the poet. Yet in his very bias toward illustrating a certain theory the poet-theorist may have done more mischief.

The passage tries – and signally fails – to preserve the New Critical sense of a firm, ontological distinction between poetry, criticism and theory. (It is to be found in William K. Wimsatt and Cleanth Brooks, *Literary Criticism: a short history* (London: Routledge & Kegan

Paul, 1957), p. 404.)

13 Paul de Man, 'The rhetoric of temporality' in Charles S. Singleton (ed.), *Interpretation: theory and practice* (Baltimore: Johns Hopkins University Press, 1969), pp. 173–209; p. 177.

14 J. Livingston Lowes. *The Road to Xanadu: a study in the ways of the imagination* (London: Pan Books, 1978). I have taken this as the most accessible edition, here and for all subsequent references.

15 ibid., p. vii.

16 See D. M. MacKinnon, 'Coleridge and Kant' in John Beer (ed.), *Coleridge's Variety: bicentenary essays* (London: Macmillan, 1974), pp. 183–293; p. 188.

17 Lowes, op. cit., p. 444.

18 ibid., p. 313.

19 ibid., p. 67.

20 ibid., p. 67.

21 See Christine Brooke-Rose, ' "The turn of the screw" and its critics: an essay in non-methodology' in Brooke-Rose, *A Rhetoric of the Unreal* (Cambridge: Cambridge University Press, 1981), pp. 128–57; p. 132.

22 Barbara Johnson, *The Critical Difference: essays in the contemporary rhetoric of reading* (Baltimore: Johns Hopkins University Press, 1980), p. xii.

23 Lowes, op. cit., p. 369.

24 See Freud's essay 'The uncanny' in *The Standard Edition of the Complete Psychological Works of Sigmund Freud*, trans. James Strachey (London: Hogarth Press, 1953–73), vol. XVII.

25 Neil Hertz, 'Freud and the sandman' in Josué V. Harari (ed.), *Textual Strategies: perspectives in post-structuralist criticism* (London: Methuen, 1979), pp. 296–321; p. 299. Jeffrey Mehlman's *Revolution and Repetition* (Berkeley and Los Angeles: University of California Press, 1979) also takes up this theme of the Freudian 'uncanny', with reference to figures of textual repetition in Marx and elsewhere.

26 Lowes, op. cit., p. 369.

27 ibid., p. 54.

28 Barbara Johnson, op. cit., p. 12.

Chapter 7

1 Gottlob Frege, 'On Sense and nominatum', trans. Herbert Feigl, in Feigl and Wilfrid Sellars (eds), *Readings in Philosophical Analysis* (New York: Appleton Century Crofts, 1949), p. 86.

2 See particularly Paul de Man, 'The epistemology of metaphor',

Critical Inquiry, vol. V (1978), pp. 13–30. On figurative language in the text of philosophy, with reference mainly to Locke and Kant.

3 See for instance Jacques Derrida, 'The supplement of Copula: philosophy *before* linguistics' in Josué V. Harari (ed.), *Textual Strategies: perspectives in post-structuralist criticism* (London: Methuen, 1979), pp. 82–120.

4 Jacques Derrida, *Writing and Difference*, trans. Alan Bass (London: Routledge & Kegan Paul, 1978), p. 160.

5 Jacques Derrida, *Of Grammatology*, trans. Gayatri Chakravorty Spivak (Baltimore and London: John Hopkins University Press, 1977) pp. 43–4.

6 Richard Rorty, *Philosophy and the Mirror of Nature* (Oxford: Basil Blackwell, 1980), p. 8.

7 ibid., p. 12.

8 W. V. O. Quine, 'Two dogmas of empiricism' in Olshewski (ed.), *Problems in the Philosophy of Language* (New York, 1969), pp. 398–417.

9 Saul Kripke, *Naming and Necessity* (second edition, revised and enlarged) (Oxford: Basil Blackwell, 1980).

10 Richard Rorty, 'Kripke versus Kant' in *London Review of Books: anthology one*, ed. Karl Miller (London: Junction Books, 1981), pp. 198–204; p. 200.

11 Kripke, op. cit., p. 39.

12 On the variations of semantic encoding for colours (specifically between English and Welsh), see Louis Hjelmslev, *Prolegomena to a Theory of Language*, trans. Francis J. Whitfield (Madison, Wisconsin: University of Wisconsin Press, 1969), pp. 53ff.

13 Michel Foucault, *The Order of Things: an archaeology of the human sciences*, trans. Alan Sheridan (London: Tavistock; New York: Pantheon, 1970).

14 Gerald Graff, *Literature against Itself: literary ideas in modern society* (Chicago and London: University of Chicago Press, 1979).

15 John R. Searle, 'Reiterating the differences' (reply to Derrida on Austin), *Glyph*, vol. I (1977), pp. 198–208.

16 Jacques Derrida, 'Limited inc abc' (response to Searle), *Glyph*, vol. II (1977), pp. 162–254.

17 Paul de Man, *Allegories of Reading: figural language in Rousseau, Nietzsche, Rilke and Proust* (New Haven and London: Yale University Press, 1979), p. 46.

18 ibid., p. 50.

19 Rorty, 'Kripke versus Kant', p. 202.

20 Ferdinand de Saussure, *Course in General Linguistics*, trans. Wade Baskin (London: Fontana/Collins, 1974), p. 71. This and subsequent passages bear witness to a general consonance of views between Saussure (placing limits on the 'arbitrary' nature of the sign) and the

Kripkean philosophy of naming. Thus: 'the only real object of linguistics is the normal, regular life of an existing idiom ... these forces of social conservation explain why the sign is unchangeable, i.e. why it resists any arbitrary substitution' (Saussure, p. 72).

21 Kripke, op. cit., p. 162.

23 Hayden White, *Metahistory: the historical imagination in nineteenth-century Europe* (Baltimore : Johns Hopkins University Press, 1973). For a further development of these themes in the context of post-structuralist theory, see White's more recent essays 'Foucault decoded' and 'The absurdist moment in contemporary literary theory'. These are reprinted in Hayden White, *Tropics of Discourse: essays in cultural criticism* (Baltimore: Johns Hopkins University Press, 1978), pp. 230–60 and 261–82.

23 Terry Eagleton, *Criticism and Ideology* (London: New Left Books, 1976). For a deconstructionist reading of this text, see Christopher Norris, *Deconstruction: theory and practice* (London: Methuen, 1982), pp. 79–83.

24 Terry Eagleton, *Walter Benjamin, or towards a revolutionary criticism* (London: New Left Books, 1981), p. 134.

25 Rorty, 'Kripke versus Kant', p. 198.

Methodological postscript

1 Susan Sontag, *Against Interpretation* (New York: Farrar, Strauss, Giroux, 1967).

2 See Roland Barthes, *The Pleasure of the Text*, trans. Richard Miller (London: Jonathan Cape, 1975).

3 For a succinct statement of this viewpoint see Tzvetan Todorov, *Introduction to Poetics*, trans. Richard Howard (Brighton: Harvester Press, 1981).

4 See particularly Jacques Derrida, 'Force and signification' in *Writing and Difference*, trans. Alan Bass (London: Routledge & Kegan Paul, 1978), pp. 3–30.

5 Roland Barthes, *S/Z*, trans. Richard Miller (London: Jonathan Cape, 1975).

6 Roland Barthes, 'Introduction à l'analyse structurale des récits', *Communications*, No. 8 (1966), pp. 1–27.

7 Jonathan Culler, *Structuralist Poetics* (London: Routledge & Kegan Paul, 1975).

8 Jonathan Culler, *The Pursuit of Signs* (London: Routledge & Kegan Paul, 1981).

9 See Rodolphe Gasché, 'Deconstruction as criticism', *Glyph*, vol. VI (1979), pp. 177–215.

10 Rodolphe Gasché, 'Unscrambling positions: on Gerald Graff's critique of deconstruction', *Modern Language Notes*, vol. XCVI (1981), pp. 1015–34.

11 Gerald Graff, *Literature Against Itself* (Chicago and London : University of Chicago Press, 1979).

12 Gerald Graff, 'Deconstruction as dogma, or, "Come back to the raft again, Strether honey"', *The Georgia Review*, vol. XXXIV (1980), p. 409.

13 Gasché, 'Unscrambling Positions', p. 1023.

14 See Jacques Derrida, 'Plato's pharmacy' in *Dissemination*, trans. Barbara Johnson (London: Athlone Press, 1982), pp. 61–171; and '. . . That dangerous supplement' in *Of Grammatology*, trans. Gayatri Chakravorty Spivak (Baltimore and London: Johns Hopkins University Press, 1977), pp. 141–64.

15 Paul de Man, *Allegories of Reading: figural language in Rousseau, Nietzsche, Rilke and Proust* (New Haven and London: Yale University Press, 1979).

16 J. Hillis Miller, *Fiction and Repetition: seven English novels* (Oxford: Basil Blackwell, 1982).

17 Jacques Derrida, 'Le facteur de la verité' in *La Carte Postale: de Socrate à Freud et au-delà* (Paris: Aubier-Flammarion, 1980), pp. 441–524.

18 Jacques Lacan, 'Seminar on "The purloined letter"', trans. J. Mehlman, *Yale French Studies*, vol. XLVIII, pp. 38-72.

19 Barbara Johnson, *The Critical Difference: essays in the contemporary rhetoric of reading* (Baltimore: Johns Hopkins University Press, 1980), p. 128.

20 Gasché, 'Unscrambling positions', p. 1024.

Name index

Subject index

(Since it figures, expressly or implicitly, as a running theme throughout
these essays, I have not thought it necessary to index the term
'deconstruction'.)